Making a Difference
How to Effect Lasting Change

Making a Difference
How to Effect Lasting Change

E.C. Nakeli

erez
Publishing
Breaking through... Breaking out

Publishing today for tomorrow's generation

© 2012 by E.C. Nakeli

Published by Perez Publishing LLC – *www.perezpublishing.com* –

For your questions and publishing needs write to:

Perez Publishing
548 Congressional Drive
Westminster, MD, 21158
USA
Email: *perezpublishing@gmail.com*

Printed in the United States of America

All rights reserved. No part of this publication may be reproduced, stored in a retrieval system, or transmitted in any form or by any means—for example, electronic, photocopy, recording—without the prior written permission of the publisher. The only exception is brief quotations in printed reviews.

E. C. Nakeli

To contact the author, write to:

E.C. Nakeli
Perez Publishing
548 Congressional Drive
Westminster, MD 21158
USA
Email: *ecnakeli@yahoo.com*

Making a Difference: How to Effect Lasting Change / E. C. Nakeli

ISBN: 978-0-9850668-3-3

Unless underwise indicated, Scripture references are from
THE HOLY BIBLE, NEW INTERNATIONAL VERSION®, NIV®
Copyright © 1973, 1978, 1984, 2011 by Biblica, Inc.™
Used by permission. All rights reserved worldwide.

Cover Image: © Cardens Design Photography Services, used by permission.

Cover/Interior Design: Zach ESSAMA - *graphicspartner@gmail.com*

Table of Contents

Dedication 7
Aknowledgement 9
Preface 11

Part I
Living Beyond Limitations 13
Chapter I: Partnership 21
Chapter II: Discipline 29
Chapter III: Freedom from the Beggar's Mentality 37
Chapter IV: Confronting Challenges 45
Chapter V: Making Use of your Assets 53
Chapter VI: Honesty and Transparency 59
Chapter VII: Power in the Name 65
Chapter VIII: The Work of Faith 69

Part II
Dealing with Unpleasant & Unwanted Situations 73

Chapter IX: Know the Techniques of the Enemy 79

Chapter X: Identify what is Feeding the Situation.................... 85

Chapter XI: Restoration and Repair.. 89

Chapter XII: Build Watch Towers in your Life.......................... 93

Chapter XIII: Reinforce your Defense 97

Chapter XIV: Arm Yourself... 101

Part III
Avoiding Compromise&Mediocrity 105

Chapter XV: The Setback of Hesitation:
Why we Resist Change 111

Chapter XVI: Flee for your Lives 117

Chapter XVII: Don't Look Back 123

Chapter XVIII: Don't Stop Anywhere in the Plain 131

Chapter XIX: Flee to the Mountain 137

Chapter XX: The Folly of the Negotiator 145

Chapter XXI: Qualification for Life on the Mountain 149

Conclusion 155

Dedication

I wholehearted, passionately, unambiguously dedicate this book to my sweetheart, the love of my life, Madeleine. You are God's timely, special, unique, and nonpareil gift to me. In a very short time you have made such a great difference in my life and world. I call you Geegee (GG) because you are God's gift to me. You are where you are today because you understood the principles of change, and what it takes to make a difference in your life and the lives of countless others. May the good Lord continue to use you in that noble profession to bring life and hope to many. I love you dearly. You are the BEST!

Aknowledgement

I wish to sincerely acknowledge my friends, Paul and Adrielle Kempa for allowing me to have my retreat in their home back in June 2011 during which I wrote this book. May the good Lord richly reward you all beyond comprehension. Thank you, Lydia Gwan for proofreading the work. Many blessings to you.

Finally, all praise goes to my Lord and King, who by the power and anointing of the Holy Spirit inspired me to write this book. Thank You Lord Jesus, for such words of divine wisdom.

Preface

Many people long for change and expect change to just happen on its own or to come looking for them. Man is the agent for change; you are the one to bring the needed change in your life and in your environment. Some people look at where they are today and wish there were something different in their today from their yesterday but unfortunately this may not be the case because they never did a thing that could have made a difference or initiate the change they needed. Is your today any different from your yesterday? Was there something you wanted to be different? Is there a change from your today you want to realize in your tomorrow? In this book we are going to look at how you can make a difference between your past and your present, your present and your future. When you understand the principles of change, you will be able to initiate change and make the needed difference. This book will be divided into three parts. In part I of the book, we will to see how you can bring about change in your life and in some other person's life by living a life that is beyond limitations. In part II we will look at how to initiate change by dealing with unpleasant and unwanted situations. In part III we are going to study how you can make a difference by avoiding compromise and mediocrity.

Part I

LIVING BEYOND LIMITATIONS

We will draw our inspiration for this part of the book from a well known passage in Acts 3:

> *1* One day Peter and John were going up to the temple at the time of prayer–at three in the afternoon. *2* Now a man crippled from birth was being carried to the temple gate called Beautiful, where he was put every day to beg from those going into the temple courts. *3* When he saw Peter and John about to enter, he asked them for money. *4* Peter looked straight at him, as did John. Then Peter said, "Look at us!" *5* So the man gave them his attention, expecting to get something from them.
> *6* Then Peter said, "Silver or gold I do not have, but what I have I give you. In the name of Jesus Christ of Nazareth, walk." *7* Taking him by the right hand, he helped him up, and instantly the man's feet and ankles became strong. *8* He jumped to his feet and began to walk. Then he went with them into the temple courts, walking and jumping, and praising God. *9* When all the people saw him walking and praising God, *10* they recognized him as the same man who used to sit begging at the temple gate called Beautiful, and they were filled with wonder and amazement at what had happened to him.
>
> (Acts 3:1-10).

The Bible is full of such passages introduced by the two-word phrase, "one day". Whenever you see any such passage you will notice that a radical change took place in someone's situation or circumstance. Every "one day" story marks the beginning of a heaven-rending, earth-shaking, ground-breaking breakthrough. "One day" is a blind date with destiny. It marks the beginning of God taking somebody from nowhere to somewhere, from under to on top. In our passage we see that this man in focus was crippled from birth. His limitation was a natural one which affected all other areas of his life. Just like he never chose the family to be born into and how he was to be born, there are many people who find themselves limited beyond their control. They find themselves in circumstances and situations brought upon them perhaps by the family they were born into or by the race they were born into, or by their country or continent of origin. Some people are under tribal or ethnic limitations. Whatever form of limitation a man or woman may be under, the sad thing is that the limitation brings additional limitations on other aspects of life. Like the subject under study his natural limitation of physical disability brought about a financial and social disability. He could not be financially independent and so he resorted to begging. There are many people who find themselves limited financially. Some are under emotional limitation, unable to express themselves emotionally; some are academically crippled or limited, unable to reach a certain scholarly level no matter how much they try. Others are socially limited, unable to rise beyond a certain socio-economic status.

A limitation is when a man or woman is unable to stand on his or her own or make any reasonable required progress in some area of their life. This cripple lived a life of meaningless routine and perpetual dependence on others. Such a state or condition makes one phony and hypocritical, reduces you to a Lilliputian, and makes you inexpressive, for fear of offending anyone. Such a scenario places you in further bondage to control, manipulation, intimidation, and fear of man which of course places you in a snare. I have seen men being enslaved by others who have let them know there is no way they can live their lives independently and succeed without them. In the Name of Jesus, I release you from any such bondage. Remember in those days, anyone with a physical defect was not allowed into the Temple courts. For this friend of ours the gate was as far as he could go. As a Jew he longed to go into the Temple to worship like his compatriots but there was a law that was limiting him. Each day he sat by the temple gates and watched other Jews walk pass him into the temple, which was the dream place for every Jew. The gate was his limit because of his physical deformity. No matter how much he desired or tried, he couldn't cross the limit of the gate. Though the gate was open and every other person walked through that open door, for him it was a closed door, permanently closed. To him the dream of worshipping in the Temple was an unattainable feat. And there are many people standing before wide open doors and you wonder why they can't go through such doors. Others are passing them and fulfilling their destinies but nothing seems to work for them. I don't know for how long you have been under that limitation. For one thing, I do not care how long you have been under. The length of your trial does not automatically imply the imminence of triumph. You will not know change until you purposefully determine and declare the end of this limitation in your life. This is the time to break the limits, overcome every barrier, and surmount every obstacle. The grace for breakthrough is available to you as you read, believe, and appropriate for yourself the freedom within your reach. The anointing of the Holy Ghost is breaking yokes and taking off limits that have hindered you until now. In the Name of Jesus, receive your deliverance from limitations. Be free!

Take Cognizance

Is there any area of your life you think you are limited or crippled in? Are you morally crippled? Are you spiritually crippled? The truth is regardless of the limitation you find yourself in, as you read through this book and believe and appropriate all that will be said here, the power of the Holy Ghost is going to terrorize and paralyze every limitation that has troubled your life. I see you free to rise to any height you so desire in life. I see every ceiling of limitation over you being carried away by the east wind of the Lord. In the Name of Jesus, I release you from the chains tying you down and holding you back. I set you free to fly like the eagle you are meant to be. The truth is the believer should live without any limitation. Not even the sky should be your limit. It is often said that the sky is your limit. But how can the sky be your limit when you have a home beyond the sky? The world says the sky is your limit because they can only see as far as the sky. As a child of God who walks by faith and not by sight, you are able to see beyond the sky unto the Throne of the Most High God. The Throne is your limit because you are seated with Christ in heavenly places. And of course Christ is seated on the Throne of majesty, which is the "limit" God has designed for you.

Your Circumstance is not Final till you Give Up

For our friend in focus, the enemy thought he had the final say in this man's life; he thought he had placed a permanent limitation over him until God showed up in his world and turned the tables. The devil doesn't have the final say; you are serving the God who is always in control, and He has showed up through this book to take you out and on top.

The question now is how can you live beyond limitations? In the chapters that follow the rest of this part, we are going to answer that question. I will share with you biblical principles on how to break every limit in life and rise to your God-ordained, Holy Ghost-engineered heights. They are simple yet effective. Through these principles I have broken every possible limitation that existed over my life.

Summary

* Every "one day" story marks the beginning of a heaven-rending, earth-shaking, ground-breaking breakthrough. "One day" is a blind date with destiny.

* Whatever form of limitation a man or woman may be under, the sad thing is that the limitation brings additional limitations on other aspects of life

* The length of your trial does not automatically imply the imminence of triumph. You will not know change until you purposefully determine and declare the end of a limitation in your life.

* As a child of God who walks by faith and not by sight, you are able to see beyond the sky unto the Throne of God. The Throne is your "limit" because you are seated with Christ in heavenly places.

* The devil doesn't have the final say; you are serving the God who is always in control, and He has showed up through this book to take you out and on top.

Chapter 1

Partnership

Our passage begins with the statement, *"one day Peter and John…"* Many people live in isolation and competition; they live even their Christian life this way, neglecting the power that is in partnership. Both Peter and John were apostles, filled with the Holy Ghost, yet they went to the Temple together to pray. This shows us that they understood the power of partnership and made use of it. Is there any doubt they shook their world and made a difference in the lives of whole communities and individuals? What would have happened had they gone to the Temple as individuals? Remember this was the first miracle they performed after the Holy Ghost had come upon them, and I believe it is this partnership that opened the door for them into the miraculous. There was an increased boldness and faith, an increase in the anointing that was present and hence the healing of the man. Partnership is a mighty tool for unlimited exploits and breakthrough. If you want to break into new territories which you may never reach as an individual, look for someone with whom you can partner. Even in obviously trivial things of your personal life as a believer, you can make strides if you tap into this latent power locked up in partnership. You can look for someone with whom to pray, study the word, fast, or evangelize. By so doing you will be developing the spiritual muscles that will enable you to eventually do those things at the personal level. Many of us don't pray as we ought to not because we do not want to but because we do not know how. The easiest way to learn how to do something is to partner with someone who already knows how to do it. The world seems to understand this principle better; that is the reason for all the mergers of large companies. They have discovered instead of competing they can make more profit by partnering with each other. Economists understand this principle; that it why some mergers are resisted by the economic watchdogs because they will gain total control of the market should the mergers be allowed. As an individual, the same power is at your disposal if you will just find the right person to partner with. Your prayer life can take a new turn. Your understanding of the Word can take a new turn for the better if you will partner with someone. Your business can take a new turn of expansion and profit if you will find the right partner. Your ministry will break into new grounds if you will find the right person to partner with.

Some Benefits of Partnership

What then are some of the benefits of partnership? How can we quantify the importance of partnership? Again let us turn to the Book for answers. This time turn with me to the book of Ecclesiastes, fourth chapter, ninth to twelfth verse:

> Two are better than one,
> because they have a good return for their labor:
> If either of them falls down,
> one can help the other up
> But pity anyone who falls

and has no one to help them up.
Also, if two lie down together, they will keep warm.
But how can one keep warm alone?
Though one may be overpowered,
two can defend themselves.
A cord of three strands is not quickly broken.

The following benefits emerge from this portion of scripture:

1. Better Return: Increase in output is one of the benefits of partnership. The results you would obtain as an individual are no match for what you could realize as a result of the right partnership. Remember the Lord told the Israelites that one of them will chase a thousand and two will chase ten thousand. In other words at the end of a partnership each person would have chased five thousand. This is five times what could have been accomplished alone. When you partner with someone your results will not only double, they will quintuple.

2. Extra Support: When you have a partner you have extra support to tap into and rely on at any moment. Partnership signifies extra resources, be they human, financial, intellectual, or material. The other person or persons in the partnership will bring in a totally different perspective and give whatever it is you are engaged in a new drive and dimension. No matter how small the other party's contribution may be, it is an addition to what you already have. Do not fail to secure the input and contribution of your partners. The Bible says in a partnership, "when one falls, the other will lift him up…" This means your partner is able to make up for your inadequacies, failures and shortcomings. The good thing about partnership is the ability to complement. David's partnership with Jonathan the son of Saul gave him extra help and support in times when he was almost giving up. In fact somehow, the partnership of David

and Jonathan was used by God to preserve David's life from relegating to the ravine of depression and despair.

3. Extra Motivation: The passage tells us two are able to keep warm when they lie together. Warmth here will signify motivation and fervor when all around will seem cold and unappealing. There are times when you need to know someone else is in this thing with you for you to continue. It is at such moments that the motivation that comes from partnership is indispensable. If you want to be honest you will agree with me that there is at least one thing you've abandoned because no one else was involved. If you had tapped into the latent power of partnership to provide a boost, you could still be going on.

4. Extra Strength: Our passage tells us that a strand of three cords is not easily broken. This means partnership provides additional strength to those involved in it. That is why when a company grows to a certain capacity, the owner may solicit the partnership of others. You are a lot stronger when somebody else has your back.

Forming a partnership with somebody does not guarantee automatic success. The principles of successful partnership must be respected and applied. Let us look at a few of such principles as revealed in the Word.

1. There must first of all be agreement. The Bible says, *"Do two walk together unless they have agreed to do so?"* (Amos 3:3). You have to agree on a working relationship and how your partnership will operate. You must agree on the goals your partnership has to realize and the methods by which the goals will be pursued, howbeit making room for flexibility and improvising as the need arises. You will have to agree on how to share the returns of the partnership. If you get into any partnership without a

clearly stated agreement, there is a high chance that conflict will ensue.

2. The partnership must take priority over individual desires within the framework of the partnership. One thing that destroys partnership is when individuals within the partnership begin to draw attention to themselves or seek personal profit at the expense of the partnership. In our passage in Acts, Peter spoke to the cripple and said, *"Look at us…"* in other words he was saying, it's a partnership, we are in this together. He could have said, *"look at me…"* After all he was the one doing the speaking, and besides he was the chief of the apostles. Peter understood that unity cannot stand when one individual in a partnership seeks to draw attention to himself. Those in partnership use the pronoun we, within the framework of the partnership than they do the pronoun I.

3. Do not impose your personal values, opinions, or conditions on others. When the cripple asked the apostles for money, Peter said to him, *"Silver or gold I do not have…"* He did not speak for John. He knew what he had and what he did not have. He allowed John to speak for himself. There are certain things you can only speak for yourself unless you are given the power of a spokesperson for the partnership. Let us conclude this segment by drawing some nuggets of wisdom from the life of Abraham. Abraham formed a partnership with a group of men and went for the rescue of Lot who had been taken captive by a group of kings (see Genesis 14:22-24). Once the battle was over and he succeeded to retrieve the plunder, the king of Sodom decided to reward him. Due to his consecration and oath to the Lord, Abraham refused any compensation. Rather, he asked that the portion of the men who went with him be allotted them. Remember that most of the men that went with him were his own

servants. Yet he refused to impose his personal values on the others though he was the leader of the group.

Having looked at partnership I want us to turn to another very important point that will help you make a difference. Partnership talks of your relationship with another but the next point will talk of your relationship with yourself. I want us to dwell next on discipline.

Summary

* Many people live in isolation and competition; they live even their Christian life this way, neglecting the power that is in partnership.

* Partnership is a mighty tool for unlimited exploits and breakthrough. If you want to break into new territory you may never reach as an individual, look for someone with whom you can partner.

* The easiest way to learn how to do something is to partner with someone who already knows how to do it.

* When you partner with someone your results will not only double; they will quintuple.

* The partnership of David and Jonathan was used by God to preserve David's life from relegating to the ravine of depression and despair.

* There are times when you need to know someone else is in this thing with you for you to continue.

* There are certain things you can only speak for yourself unless you were given the power of a spokesperson for the partnership.

* Those in partnership use the pronoun "we," within the framework of the partnership, rather than the pronoun "I."

Chapter II

Discipline

Discipline is threefold in the sense in which I'll use it here; it is doing what you have to do, how you have to do it, when you have to do it. It is an indispensable quality for those who must make a difference from their yesterday and bring change to their tomorrow. I have seen great potentials buried in the grave of indulgence, complacency, and self-sparing. On the other hand, I have seen less gifted people accomplish feats that can only be credited to their discipline.

Our passage tells us that Peter and John were going to the Temple at the time of prayer. They were men whose lives were marked by discipline. They were going to pray at the time of prayer. They knew what to do and how to do it. People who make a difference between their today and tomorrow are those who have a sense of priority. They know what must be given the first place in their daily routines. I have come to realize that men who make a difference in their time are men of dynamic routines. Note that I said dynamic routines; that is, such people have a sense of routine yet are not bound by such routines, they are flexible enough to make adjustments when necessary. There are people bound by a ritual of static routine, their focus is the routine and not the product or effect of the former. With a dynamic routine you keep to the routine as long as it is producing the required results and are willing to adapt as the need may arise. Such were the apostles. They were disciplined enough to establish a dynamic routine in the business of prayer.

We said discipline consists of three aspects: doing what you have to do, how you have to do it, when you have to do it. Let us look at how each will help you make a difference and bring change to your life and environment.

Doing what you Have to Do

To do what you have to do means you've got to know what you have to do in order to do it. The effectiveness of your life is not measured by the volume of what you do. Many people are doing a lot of things yet are neglecting the very thing that matters most to them, namely what they are supposed to be doing. What you are supposed to do are things which are in line with your calling or assignment. They are things of primary importance to the realization of your dreams and visions. Opportunities are evaluated with respect to their impact on the big picture when you know what you have to do and are engaged in doing it. This is where the power of planning comes in. It is written in the Book that *"But the noble make noble plans, and by noble deeds they stand."* (Isaiah 32:8) In other words what takes you into nobility and what keeps you in nobility is your ability to make noble plans which lead to noble deeds. You must ask yourself important questions with respect to the big picture and decide on the things you must do within the next hour, day, week, month, year, decade and so on, to help you realize the big picture. I want you to put this message into practice right away. Take a pen and a paper and write reasonable, concrete, and measurable things you intend to do within the next hour, day, week, month, and year with respect to what you want to do with your life. I said measurable because you will need to evaluate after each time frame whether you did accomplish your goals; if you did not find out what the deterrents were and how can they be overcome.

Making plans causes you to evaluate things and opportunities with respect to their contribution to the realization of those plans. There are some good and pleasant things you will have to say, "no" to because they will divert time and resources from that which matters and must be done. Have you not realized that people who have made a difference in their world are sometimes considered weird or controversial? People do not understand why they wouldn't engage in certain activities or go to certain places, or spend on certain things. To make a difference in your today or tomorrow, to bring change to your life, know what you have to do and do it.

Knowing how to Do it

This is another important factor to take into consideration in the measure of discipline. It does not suffice to do what you have to do; you will have to do it how it must be done, that is, the method which is most effective and efficient. This may vary with individuals, and no one can better discover how you can do certain things with maximum efficiency and effectiveness but yourself. Some things have a standard way of doing them, others, not so much. The methods used may vary with people's gifts, talents, and callings. When you know what you have to do and how you have to do it and follow through, it will keep you from disorderliness and wastefulness. You will maximize the use of your time and other resources. Knowing your methods will reveal to you the equipment and personnel you need. Again it will require flexibility, establishing a dynamic routine.

Knowing when to Do it

Time is another important factor in the definition of discipline, if not the most important. Many people know what they have to do, and how they have to do it but fail to do it when they have to because of poor time management. The Bible says God has made everything beautiful in its time. This means there are things which can only produce their best results within a certain time frame. Out of that time frame their effect becomes minimal and negligible. Remember there is a time for everything (see Ecclesiastes 3). The thing about time is that it always appears abundantly available until you set out to do what you have to do and realize that there is no time, at least not as much as you thought. The difference between those who have excelled and those who have produced mediocre results can be traced not to their abilities but to their sense of time management. And good time management is just doing what you have to do when you have to do it, for the duration you have to do it.

In writing to his disciple Timothy, towards the end of his second letter, Paul told him, *"Do your best to come to me before winter"* (2 Timothy 4:21a). In this short sentence there are two very important principles of discipline I'll like us to look at:

Do your Best

Discipline involves doing the best you can, using all you have to see something accomplished. To make the difference does not require you to be the best but it requires you to be at your best no matter how mundane the task may be. The supernatural help and support of God is available to those who are doing their best. You are not in need of extra support if you are not using all you are supposed to. This entails hard work and commitment to excellence. Your best does not come out until you consciously decide to give it your best efforts. Doing your best will mean sparing nothing that can be used in the process of executing a task, thereby maximizing effectiveness and efficiency.

Set Deadlines

Paul told Timothy to do his best to come before winter. That was setting a deadline. If you are to bring change to your life and your world, you will have to set deadlines for yourself. If you do not set deadlines for yourself, it is likely that you will drift into the pit of procrastination. And there are many people trapped in this pit not knowing how to come out of it. The way to prevent being trapped in this bottomless pit is for you to work with this principle of personal deadlines. It will help you maximize the use of your time and keep you focused. It will also help you do away with distracting activities that steal your attention and enable you pull all your resources towards the execution of your priorities.

Summary

* I have seen great potential buried in the grave of indulgence, complacency, and self-sparing. On the other hand, I have seen less gifted people accomplish feats that can only be credited to their discipline.

* People who make a difference between their today and tomorrow are those who have a sense of priority. They know what must be given the first place in their daily routines.

* With a dynamic routine you keep to the routine as long as it is producing the required results and are willing to adapt as the need may arise.

* Discipline consists of three aspects: doing what you have to do, how you have to do it, and when you have to do it.

* Opportunities are evaluated with respect to their impact on the big picture when you know what you have to do and are engaged in doing it.

* There are some good and pleasant things you will have to say no to because they will divert time and resources from that which matters and must be done.

* When you know what you have to do and how you have to do it and follow through, it will keep you from disorderliness and wastefulness. You will maximize the use of your time and other resources.

* The difference between those who have excelled and those who have produced mediocre results can be traced not to their abilities but to their sense of time management.

* To make a difference does not require you to be the best but it requires you to be at your best no matter how mundane the task may be.

* The supernatural help and support of God is available to those who are doing their best.

* If you do not set deadlines for yourself, it is likely that you will drift into the pit of procrastination.

Chapter III

Freedom from the Beggar's Mentality

The foremost characteristic of a beggar is that he or she depends totally on the mercy and generosity of others. A beggar accepts whatever is given him or her. In other words a beggar takes life as it comes without any effort to change things. And there are many people living with this kind of mentally that says I accept whatever life has offered me. When people ask me, *"how is life treating you?"* I always respond by saying I treat life and never allow life to treat me. When you allow life to treat you, it can treat you very cruelly. Beggars are those who have accepted life to dictate what happens to them. A beggar's mentality is the mentality of slavery and bondage. Like I said in the opening pages of this part of the book, when you are dependent on others, there is high probability that you will be phony and hypocritical because you wouldn't want to express your opinion lest you offend those on whom you depend. Those with a beggarly mentality lose their identity by trying to squeeze into the mold of what their environment has forced on them. The beggar's mentality makes you always want to blame others for the situation in which you find yourself. Some blame their parents, others their children, others their spouse, others their former boss, others their pastor or leader. They see everything wrong with others and nothing wrong with themselves. It is the mentality that says because A did not do this for me, this or that which was supposed to happen failed to happen; beggars are good at the blame game. They live in resentment and bitterness towards those they consider the agent of their misfortune.

Another sad thing is that while there are people genuinely qualify to beg because of an adverse physical or mental disability, you find some with potentials and useful talent who are also living the beggarly lifestyle. Many people with great ability have been held captive and grounded by the beggar's mentality and therefore have become liabilities instead of the assets God made them to be. It is the beggar's mentality that makes us think we should perpetually be employed by others even when we have the potential and resources to create jobs and become employers. So we stick to employment even when the employers are abusive and unappreciative of us. I have no problem working for somebody provided I am satisfied and contented with it and I do not consider myself unfairly treated. For some, being employed by others was meant to be just a starter and nothing else. The unfortunate thing is that what was meant to jumpstart them in life has been converted into a livelihood.

What is the Beggar's Mentality?

The beggar's mentality is that which says poverty is a blessing, and believes that God has destined some people to live in perpetual poverty. The fact that you were born poor is no excuse to live and die poor. Your ancestors may be responsible for your yesterday but they are definitely not responsible for your today and your tomorrow. You can make a difference and change the story of your life and of another's by breaking free from the beggar's mentality. The beggar's mentality is the mentality of losers who see no hope or possibility of change. In the Name of Jesus the Christ, I set you free from the beggar's mentality. I release you from bondage to an unregenerate mind.

How to Be Free from the Beggar's Mentality

To be permanently and totally free form the beggar's mentality, you must change the way you think and begin to view opportunities in your disappointments, possibilities in the apparently impossible. I separate you from the idea that you cannot succeed unless you lose your identity to put on another's. I have seen people who have been maltreated and abused, and misused and can do nothing about it because they've been brainwashed to believe their destiny depends on a human being. It is true that sometimes God uses people to bring us to our new level, but the truth is those assigned by God to help us fulfill our destinies never try to exploit or enslave people to themselves. To free yourself from this enslaving mentality you must take your eyes off man and lift them up to the throne from where true help comes.

God in His sovereignty has used many people to move me from one level to another. Sometimes promotion has come from unexpected quarters. There are people, even very close relatives who owed it to my parents to be of help to me but failed to because I refused to buy their idea of losing my identity to put on theirs. Some who had the opportunity to be part of God's great plan for my life threw it away because they figured out I was not willing to be enslaved, first of all in my thinking, and secondly in my actions. One of the problems I had with my father while growing up is that I always wanted to be financially independent. I did many odd jobs as a kid just to make my own money. Many times I got beaten for working to earn money but when he realized that I would not be stopped he gave in and helped me secure "better jobs". This was an asset to me when things started going down financially for the family. I had learned to work with my hands. Many times I paid my own school fees. I went to school in the morning and worked in the evening and during holidays. I decided that I will not be trapped in the poverty that was all around me at that stage in life. While my childhood friends were blaming their parents and relatives for their predicament, I was investing in my future. My dad gave us the best when he had the means; that is why he never allowed us to go to some other person's house for holidays, or to work when things were up and going financially for him. But the sad thing is that some of my siblings and relatives are still bitter against him, in spite of his best efforts. The beggar's mentality still keeps them bound as they whine about some other person's past, and unknown to them, they are being drifted in the sea of purposelessness. Again the truth is your parents are not the problem; your former company is not the problem; your government is not the issue either; your mentality and beliefs are! Face the truth and free yourself in the Name of Jesus.

Your Appearance Matters

Peter and John could bring change into this beggar's life because they themselves were free from the beggar's mentality. They knew that this man was not created by God to be a beggar. Though the apostles here didn't have a dime in their pockets, surely the beggar mistook them for rich guys, that is why he could ask them for money. There are some people whom you see even from a distance and can draw a conclusion that they do not have a dime in their pockets. Some people carry their poverty on the placard of their appearance and language. The apostles were well dressed and looked presentable even in the absence of money. We all know the value of a thing is greatly affected by its presentation, and people will value you according to how you present yourself. A beggarly appearance does not make you spiritual and more consecrated. If anything it makes you look ludicrous even before angels, who often wonder why a child of the King of the universe should be bound by such a mentality. Some people beg even in their prayers forgetting to know that the Father has invited us to ask and not to beg. They beg their circumstances, beg their sin, and beg the devil to let them go. It sounds like humility when you pray and beg but it is actually the foolishness of the beggar's mentality. Your father says you should ask, wherever you brought that beggar's mentality and language from, let it go. Free yourself from the language and choices of a beggar. This starts by you acknowledging and receiving what God has decreed about you. You can read my book, "<u>105 Things God Says About You</u>". It will transform and renew your mind, and give you a prince's perspective about life.

Summary

* When you allow life to treat you, it can treat you very cruelly.

* Those with a beggarly mentality lose their identity by trying to squeeze into the mold of what their environment has forced on them.

* Many people with great abilities have been held captive and grounded by the beggar's mentality and therefore have become liabilities instead of the assets God has made them to be.

* The fact that you were born poor is no excuse to live and to die poor. Your ancestors may be responsible for your yesterday but they are definitely not responsible for your today and your tomorrow.

* You can make a difference and change the story of your life and that of another by breaking free from the beggar's mentality.

* To free yourself from this enslaving mentality you must take your eyes off man and lift them up to the throne from where true help comes.

* The truth is your parents are not the problem; your former company is not the problem; your government is not the issue either; your mentality and beliefs are! Face the truth and free yourself in the Name of Jesus.

* A beggarly appearance does not make you spiritual and more consecrated. If anything is makes you look ludicrous even before angels.

* We all know the value of a thing is greatly affected by its presentation, and people will value you according to how you present yourself.

Chapter IV

Confronting Challenges

While some are bound by the beggar's mentality, others are bound by the runaway or escapee mentality. They run from challenges and become fugitives from themselves because they do not want to face reality. Problems don't resolve themselves; neither do challenges cease to exist because you cower from facing them. The challenge you flee today will be there to face you tomorrow with greater resolve. The truth is any challenge you refuse to face is only postponed while you mark time and fail to make the progress you ought.

For Peter and John, facing this crippled beggar with empty pockets was a challenge. Perhaps they would have changed their route to the temple, or ignored the man's plea for money because they wanted to avoid an embarrassing situation that exposed the fact that they were penniless. They could also have opted to reproach the man by asking him why he spent his whole life begging instead of doing something useful with is own hands. We just enumerated various ways some people escape from reality:

- They do everything to avoid any face to face contact with the issue in question.
- They ignore the issue as though it were nonexistent.
- They create other problems that cover the real issue.
- They admit the problem and the need to deal with it but keep postponing the resolution.
- They pretend the problem is solved.
- They claim to have other issues of greater priority.

When Peter and John met this challenge, they refused to shy from it; they faced it; they looked it in the eye and addressed it. Our passage tells us that, *"Peter looked straight at him, as did John."* They faced the issue squarely in the face in spite of the fact that they had no money to offer the man. By facing this challenge, they leaped into a totally new dimension in their ministry and made a difference in someone else's life.

With every challenge you refuse to face, you forfeit an opportunity for growth. By shying away from challenges you also discard the promotion that comes with addressing and overcoming challenges. Israel remained in the desert for forty years because they refused to face the challenge of the giants in the Promised Land. The army of Israel under King Saul, armed and ready for war, ran from the challenge of facing Goliath until David stepped in and won the battle against Goliath, bringing freedom to God's people. David was bold enough to look the challenge in the eye and address it with the Word of God; this opened a door to a totally new dimension of his life. It is time for believers to rise up and look in the eye of what has kept them in bondage and address such with the Word of God. Words are not enough to challenge your challenges; the armor of Saul is not what you need either. You need to be armed with your own "sling and stone". Note that what gave David courage and inspiration to confront this particular challenge was the fact that he had confronted and dealt with earlier challenges by the names of a bear and a lion. Those who are consistent in dealing with smaller challenges in life are building their confidence to deal with the determinant challenges of the future. Had David built the habit of running away, he sure would have ran away from this one too, and by so doing remained a shepherd boy his entire life.

Confront Yourself

Are there some realities and challenges you are running from facing? Will you decide to address those challenges? If you do not, chances are you will stay at the level you are at the moment.

The Lord Jesus knew we were going to face challenges. That's why He said, *"if you say to this mountain be removed and…"* Mountains are challenges and you have to address them for them to be dealt with. The Lord has made you a promise, saying:

> See, I will make you into a threshing sledge,
> new and sharp, with many teeth.
> You will thresh the mountains and crush them,
> and reduce the hills to chaff.
> You will winnow them, the wind will pick them up,
> and a gale will blow them away.
> But you will rejoice in the LORD
> and glory in the Holy One of Israel
>
> (Isaiah 41:15-16).

God has made you one before whom challenges will bow as you step out to face them. He has said you are going to be a thresher and crusher of mountains. You must know and believe this and decide to run from no challenge in life that needs to be confronted. On the other side of every challenge is a change. As you overcome the challenge you will be stepping into change in some area of your life. Every challenge you face today and overcome strengthens you and makes you a master over that challenge. I face my challenges with this promise because when the Lord called me, He used this passage to speak and to reassure me of victory and success.

In another passage the Lord has promised,

> I will lead the blind by ways they have not known,
> along unfamiliar paths I will guide them;
> I will turn the darkness into light before them
> and make the rough places smooth.
> These are the things I will do;
> I will not forsake them
>
> (Isaiah 42:16).

In the above passage, we see the Lord describing several categories of challenges that will confront you as you move towards fulfilling your destiny:

The Challenge of the Unknown

This is the challenge that presents itself each time you want to move into new territory. The way to confront and deal with such challenges is to trust and rely on the leadership of the Holy Spirit. He has promised to lead the blind by ways unknown to them. This means you are not depending on your ability to see or on your past experience since this is a way you have not known before. Following the leadership of the One who knows every way and sees the end from the beginning is the only sure way to overcome challenges of the unknown. Be willing and ready to step into the unknown. Therein lies the power to overcome and orchestrate reasonable and measurable change.

The Challenge of the Unfamiliar

Many of us enjoy dealing only with territories we are familiar with. Some territories, we have been there once or twice but they are still unfamiliar to us in one way or another. And we dread stepping into such territories especially when our first attempt was not a pleasant one. We confront these challenges by trusting His guidance and direction. Often, treading the unfamiliar path is the gateway to life-changing discoveries. Some people's names are engraved in the annals of human history just because they trod that unfamiliar path which others were afraid to.

The Challenge of the Uncertain (Darkness)

Darkness here refers to that which is uncertain and unclear. Often the challenges that bring the greatest breakthrough and change are those which come with a lot of risks. Even for these kinds of challenges, God has promised us His light of revelation as a solution. As you step into the dark, trust the light of revelation to light up the darkness. Remember that His word is a lamp to your feet and a light unto your path. Thus, again we see the Word of God being very vital in confronting the challenges of life. Sometimes in life the only thing you can be certain of is the fact that there is a God who is faithful and who is in absolute control. You do not need many certainties to effect lasting change; you need divine approval and assurance.

The Challenge of the Unavoidable

Perhaps the path you are treading is a known and familiar path to you, everything seems clear and certain, yet even for this there are challenges of its own. For every path there are the rough places, the twisted and sharp bends which you must decide to face. For some people even when it is evident that there is success and change on the other side, they are just still too scared to confront their challenges.

Their problem is the fear of pain or temporary loss. Be willing to take up the unavoidable.

Regardless of the form your challenge assumes, the solution will come as you set out in boldness to confront it. It is as you step into the unknown that God's leadership comes. It is as you step into the unfamiliar that you get His guidance. It is as you step into darkness that you get the light of revelation. It is as you step on the rough path that He smooths it out. I declare freedom for you from the fear of facing challenges. I deliver you from being a fugitive from reality, in the Name of Jesus Christ.

Summary

* While some are bound by the beggar's mentality, others are bound by the runaway or escapee mentality. They run from challenges and become fugitives from themselves because they do not want to face reality.

* Problems don't resolve themselves; neither do challenges cease to exist because you cower before them. The challenge you escape today will face you tomorrow with a greater resolve.

* With every challenge you refuse to face, you forfeit an opportunity for growth. By shying away from challenges you also reject the promotion that comes with confronting and overcoming them.

* David's resolve to look the challenge of Goliath in the eye and address it with the Word of God opened the door to a totally new dimension of his life.

* Those who are consistent in dealing with smaller challenges in life are building their confidence to deal with the determinant challenges of the future.

* God has made you one before whom challenges will bow as you step out to face them. He has said you are going to be a thresher and crusher of mountains.

* Be willing and ready to step into the unknown. Therein lies the power to overcome and orchestrate reasonable and measurable change.

* Often, treading unfamiliar path is the gateway to life-changing discoveries. Some people's names are engraved in the annals of human history just because they trod that unfamiliar path which others were afraid to.

* Sometimes in life the only thing you can be certain of is the fact that there is a God who is faithful and who is in absolute control. You do not need many certainties to effect lasting change; you need divine approval and assurance.

Chapter V

Making Use of your Assets

We live in a world that concentrates on the negative, and this has had its effect on those who live in it. It is easier to cry over what you do not have than to rejoice over what you have. It is easier to see a glass half-empty than to see it half-full. We have been wired to notice that which is lacking. That's why when you walk in the flesh it is easier to behold the weaknesses of people rather than their strength. You easily find reason to criticize and castigate rather than appreciate and celebrate. For you to effect change and make a difference you need to first of all realize what you have and begin making use of it. If you spend your time mourning over what you do not have instead of celebrating what you have, the chances are high that you'll continue to maintain the status quo.

What Can you Offer?

The truth is everybody has something to offer in this life, something that can effect change even in a small dimension. The moment you think you have nothing to offer you start seeing yourself as good-for-nothing, which makes you unproductive. For the crippled beggar, though he had no legs to carry him about he had his mouth to ask people to carry him to his place of begging daily. Though he was at the place of begging, even there he had something to give. The Bible says when Peter told him to look at them, *"the man **gave** them his attention"*. It may not have been significant to make him walk but it was all he had to give. And because he gave what he had, he could receive what he needed. An unprecedented change and difference was brought into his life just by him using what he had. Peter told him, "…such as I have…" Peter did not have silver or gold, but he knew what he had, the name of Jesus, and made use of it. This brought change into the cripple's life and in Peter's ministry. He was launched into a totally different dimension of supernatural miracles. Listen to me please; you already have what is needed to bring change to your circumstance. It may be at an undiscovered, unexploited, rudimentary stage but you already have it. You may not like it but it is what you need to move to your next level. It is what you need to distinguish yourself from the masses. Look at Bible history and you will discover that those whom God has used to bring change to their world needed nothing in addition to what they already had. All that was needed was the blessing of God upon it.

What you Have Can Make a Difference

Moses had his shepherd staff. Through the years, he unwittingly held in his hands the tool to be used of God to bring freedom to an entire nation. Surely Moses did not know what contribution his staff was going to play in his destiny. When God asked him, "what is that in your hand?" He was pointing out to Moses that he already had all that was needed for God to use him to change the world around him. When he and the Israelites were stuck at the Red Sea, Moses cried out to God; God asked him, *"why are you crying out to me?"* He then instructed him to make use of the staff that was in his hand to divide the Red Sea. You may have been crying out to God for a miracle, but what you need is actually in your own hands. Use it to divide your Red Sea and move to the next level of your life. Refuse to be stuck at your Red Sea because of what you do not have. Look at what you have and make use of it.

Samson came face to face with a band of enemy soldiers with no weapon in his hands. The only thing he had in his immediate environment was a jawbone. Instead of fretting for the lack of weapons, he actually made use of the jawbone to slay a thousand men. Look, God wants to use what you already have. Stop looking left and right for what you do not have. There is something right where you are, something you must use to bring you victory and take you to your next level.

The prophet's widow who came running to Elisha to bail her out of the situation of debt her late husband left her in did not realize God was going to make use of the *"just a little oil"* she had in her house. God used nothing but a little oil to bail her out and change the story of her life. David used nothing else but his sling and shot to overcome the challenge of Goliath. God wants to use what you present to Him to bring about the needed change in your life and environment. He wants to place His hand of blessing on it and make it an agent of change, first of all in your own life, then in your environment. The problem is that we keep to ourselves what should be offered to God for use. We refuse to place at His disposal our staff, our little oil, our five loaves and two fish.

Take the Step

I want you to make an inventory of your gifts, talents, special abilities, and other resources that are at your disposal. Write down across each gift, talent, special skill or resource, ways in which you think these can be of benefit to your environment. Which of these do you think is most likely to succeed? I do not mean which of them will bring you the most fame or gain. No, I mean which of them can easily impact the lives of the people around you? It may not be the most profitable but it may be the stepping stone to your next level. Remember you can always use what you have to get what you want. The problem with most people is that they want to start big, forgetting to know that Rome was not built in a day. Find out how you can put these gifts to use for the benefit of the people around you. By doing this you are putting to use what you have, thereby paving the way for change. Remember, the Bible says a man's gift will make a way for him.

Summary

* For you to effect change and make a difference you need to first of all realize what you have and begin making use of it.

* Because the cripple at the Temple gate gave what he had, he could receive what he needed. An unprecedented change and difference was brought into his life just by him using what he had.

* Those whom God has used to bring change to their world needed nothing in addition to what they already had. All that was needed was the blessing of God upon it.

* When God asked him, "what is that in your hand?" He was drawing our attention to the fact that just like Moses, we already have all that He needs to use us to make a difference in our world.

* Refuse to be stuck at your Red Sea because of what you do not have. Look at what you have and make use of it.

* Stop looking left and right for what you do not have. There is something right where you are needed to bring you victory and take you to your next level.

* God wants to use what you present to Him to bring about the needed change in your life and environment. He wants to place His hand of blessing on it and make

it an agent of change, first of all in your own life, then in your environment.

* Remember you can always use what you have to get what you want. The problem with most people is that they want to start big, forgetting to know that Rome was not built in a day.

Chapter VI

Honesty and Transparency

We live in a world of duplicity and covertness, with people taking unfair advantage of others. In the world today it pays to cheat and exploit others for personal gain and promotion. People who live like this cannot make a true difference in their environment. The kind of change and difference we have been talking about is the one that goes beyond self to the benefit of others. True change can never be made by exploiting others or taking unfair advantage of them.

Honesty is a virtue that those who must effect real change must find and hold on to. Sadly, in a system where everything but honesty is encouraged there are few who believe being honest can help you make a difference. You can be one of the few, which in itself can make a difference. When our cripple friend asked the apostles for money, Peter was honest to say he did not have any money. Peter did not pretend to not hear the man's request, but said, *"silver or goal I do not have..."* By being honest to own up for what he did not have, his eyes could only but turn to what he had. The reason why some people fail to make use of what they have is because they are not honest to acknowledge what they do not have; they spend all their time brooding over what is lacking in their lives. You cannot effect change and make any difference that way!

It's not Always Wrong to Say no!

Another aspect of honesty is the ability to say no. When you are honest to say no when you have to, it will save you a great deal of energy and resources that are often wasted trying to do things for which you are not equipped to do. You can be amazed at how many people fail because they attempted doing things they knew from the onset were not going to succeed but went ahead anyway because someone or some system expected it from them. Be honest and willing to say I do not have what is takes to do that which has been demanded or is expected of me. Think of all the resources that are wasted attempting projects that will obviously fail because those in it were not honest with themselves and with their sponsors! Honesty will mean you saying, *"Please I do not have the ability or skill it will take to do this, is there someone better placed to do it?"* Another evil in these last days of spiritual supermen is that you find people who do everything and function in all the ministries and hence the ineffectiveness and inefficiencies that are plaguing the church. Some people believe they are the embodiment of spiritual gifts and therefore see no reason for the ministries of others. By this, churches are limited and fail to make the difference and produce the needed impact in their environment. There are things you see some people do and you know in your heart it is not something they were supposed to be doing. Be honest enough to say, *"That is not my calling, the Holy Spirit has not equipped me for that or called me to do that"*. What breeds such dishonesty is the spirit of competition and self-sufficiency. Even Paul the great apostle said he was not called to baptize but to preach the Gospel. In other words he was saying he knew what he had been equipped to do.

Be Bold

There are some who believe they are to be the messiah of others. The Lord has called us to bear each other's burden, and it is often a joy when we are privileged to offer help to fellow humans. However, some have misunderstood this to mean they have to meet every need they come across. They get into debt to try to help others. This is nothing but folly. When you have given all you have, then that is all you can give for the sake of others. Be honest to say I do not have the additional resources it will take to meet these other needs. And if God wants you to meet those needs He will make a way for you without you needing to get yourself entangled in debt. Do not allow yourself to crumble under the crushing weight of man-imposed burdens because you are not bold and honest enough to say you can take no more responsibility. God has not made you a spiritual superman. If you break and abuse spiritual and physical laws because of dishonesty, you will be the first to suffer for it. As a young bank manager, I was often caught in a place of overwhelming demand on me by men and women who thought all the money in the bank was my personal money; they failed to understand that I too had a limited salary from which I could only offer help this far. Many times I found myself in the hard place of needing to say no to the genuine and pressing demands of people, whether they were on my personal finances or on the finances of the institution for which I was branch head. I had pastors coming to me from left to right because they knew I was a fellow pastor, to make demands for loans for which they never qualified. Again I had to be determined to say no. This spared me a lot of trouble with colleagues in the ministry, though it was often not an easy decision to take. It is true that in some cases I used my discretion and offered personal help where possible. Another positive reward of honestly saying no is that it keeps you from making expenditures for money you do not have at present or will have in the nearest future. Do not give to impress or *"sacrifice"* out of the desire to win the applause of men.

Be Transparent

Another way to ensure that you live honestly is to be transparent in your dealings with others. Peter told the beggar, *"look at us…"* Now when you ask someone to look at you, you sure are telling that person to examine you. Live your life at any moment such that when people look at you they will find nothing shady in you dealings and affairs with others. You cannot make any permanent change or difference when you live with skeletons in your closet. In a society where gossip and scrutiny are heavy money-making industries you cannot afford to have all your labor come crashing before you simply because of some shady transactions of yours. Are you living in such a way that when your financial dealings are scrutinized it will reveal nothing illicit? Are you living in such a way that your relations are pure and uphold moral probity? Forget a double life if you are to make any lasting and permanent impact in the world of today. Do not undo the impact of your life through involvement in shady transactions. Walk in the light always and shun darkness and shady dealings.

Summary

* True change can never be effected by exploiting others or taking unfair advantage of them.

* Honesty is a virtue that those who must effect real change must find and hold on to.

* The reason why some people fail to make use of what they have is because they are not honest to acknowledge what they do not have.

* When you are honest to say no when you have to, it will save you a great deal of energy and resources that are often wasted trying to do things for which you are not equipped.

* Another evil in these last days is that of spiritual supermen who try to do everything and function in all the ministries, hence the ineffectiveness and inefficiencies that are plaguing the church.

* Do not allow yourself to crumble under the crushing weight of man-imposed burdens because you are not bold and honest enough to say you can take no more responsibility. God has not made you a spiritual superman.

* You cannot make any permanent change or difference when you live with skeletons in your closet.

* Forget a double life if you are to make any lasting and permanent impact in the world of today. Do not undo the impact of your life by involvement in shady transactions. Walk in the light always and shun dark and shady dealings.

Chapter VII

Power in the Name

The Name of Jesus, spoken under the anointing of the Holy Spirit is the most potent weapon available to every saint to effect change and make a difference. The problem is that many of us have fallen short of understanding the tremendous power that is released when that Name is mentioned in faith and expectation. This lack of understanding has made us to fail to use the Name as often as we ought, and in circumstances we are supposed to. The Name of Jesus is the universal key to unlock every door that must be unlocked to usher you to your next level. It is the bulldozer you need to remove any barrier placed by the evil one on your path to fulfilling your destiny. Apart from the Holy Spirit, the Name of Jesus is the greatest gift Christ left His bride as an agent of change here on planet earth. It is the instrument we use to see His Kingdom come and His will done on earth as it is in heaven.

Peter told the cripple, *"...but such as I have, in the Name of Jesus, rise up and walk..."* Saint you need to discover the power that is in that Name. The Name of Jesus is what gave the cripple new legs and changed him from one who couldn't enter the Temple courts to one who now was jumping and leaping and testifying to the healing power in the Name. When the apostles were being questioned after their arrest by the religious leaders of their day for healing a man, Peter told them, *"If we are being called to account today for an act of kindness shown to a man who was lame and are being asked how he was healed, then know this, you and all the people of Israel: It is by the name of Jesus Christ of Nazareth, whom you crucified but whom God raised from the dead, that this man stands before you healed."* (Acts 4:9-10) The Name of Jesus gave this guy new legs, new bones, new ankles, and a new story.

The name of Jesus is meant to bring us deliverance, healing, provision, salvation, protection, breakthrough, promotion, contentment and every other thing you think you need to make a difference in your life and in your world. The Name of Jesus is the passcode to the release of the power of the Almighty God. When you pronounce the Name in faith and under the anointing all of heaven pays attention to what is being requested, and hell is forced into a position of obeisance. I have seen that Name bring deliverance when nothing else would. I have seen it work miracles of healing and provision. I have seen that Name bring deliverance in times of emergency. Oh the Name of Jesus! It is a strong tower, a refuge, a fortress in times of storm. By that name armies are put into confusion and flight; demons are bound and cast out of people and territories. The Name is what has taken me from one level of my life to another. It has brought me favor where I would otherwise have gotten none. It has opened doors for me which would have remained permanently shut. In a sense, that Name is all I've got and I hold the Name and the One who has it in high esteem. It is your trump card in times of danger and distress. The Name of Jesus is meant to bring salvation not only from sin but from embarrassing situations and circumstances. It brings direction when you need it, gives you peace in the midst of chaos, and keeps you hopeful when all seems fading. That Name is able to make you bold and fearless in the face of adversity and give you strength when you are weak and can't carry on. The Bible says every knee must bow to that Name, every tongue must confess the Lordship of the Name. Every other name must submit to the power and authority of the Name. One thing that makes me glad and confident about the Name of Jesus is that the Name has both power and authority locked up in it, power and authority that are released each time we mention the Name in faith. Because of this, everything that will not respect the authority of that Name will bow to the power of the Name.

Summary

* The Name of Jesus, spoken under the anointing of the Holy Spirit is the most potent weapon available to every saint to effect change and make a difference.

* The Name of Jesus is the universal key to unlock every door that must be unlocked to usher you to your next level.

* Apart from the Holy Spirit, the Name of Jesus is the greatest gift Christ left His bride as an agent of change here on planet earth. It is the instrument we use to see His Kingdom come and His will done on earth as it is in heaven.

* The name of Jesus is meant to bring us deliverance, healing, provision, salvation, protection, breakthrough, promotion, contentment and every other thing you think you need to make a difference in your life and in your world.

* The Name of Jesus is the passcode to the release of the power of the Almighty God. When you pronounce the Name in faith and under the anointing all of heaven pays attention to what is being requested, and hell is forced into a position of obeisance.

* In a sense, that Name is all I have got and I hold the Name and the One who has it in high esteem. It is your trump card in times of danger and distress.

Chapter VIII

The Work of Faith

This is the most vital step that determines if you will live above limitations or not. After confronting your challenges, you must step out and act in faith. Peter looked at the cripple and said, "In the Name of Jesus Christ of Nazareth, walk." Peter gave a faith command to the cripple to walk but did not end there. He had to put his faith to work by reaching out to the man and grabbing him by the hand. The problem with many of us is that we end at the level of declaring, and proclaiming, and prophesying, and praying. Peter did something additional to the faith command he gave. It is clear that Peter did not see an immediate result of the man jumping up and walking after he commanded him to, in the name of Jesus. It is at this point that many have given up on breaking the barriers of limitation that stands before them; it is here that many have cowered and backed away from the challenges that stand before them. It was not the case for Peter. We are told that, *"Taking him by the right hand, he helped him up, and instantly the man's feet and ankles became strong. He jumped to his feet and began to walk."* The results were only realized when Peter began acting and putting his faith to work. The breakthrough you have been waiting for may be waiting for you to act. The miracle you have been expecting may be expecting you to make a move. What if grabbing the man by the hand did not help him stand? What if the man fell? Peter was willing to take his chances and put his faith to work.

Take a Look Around

You can effect change and make a difference in someone else's life by putting your faith to action. There are many people around whom you can reach out to and help by putting your faith to work. You can reach out to a person in need while trusting God for provision. Change has come to many people and a difference made in different circumstances because someone decided against all odds and contrary evidence to put his faith to work. The change that came into this man's life and world after his limitation was taken away was remarkable; it could not be ignored by anyone who met him. The Temple gate was no longer a limit for him as we read that *"he went with them into the Temple courts."* He could now walk through the open door that had seemed shut to him for many years. He now realized the dream of every Jew–worshipping in the Temple of the Great Jehovah. Only this time around he did not need anybody to carry him around. He was walking and jumping and praising God. His weakness had been turned to strength. When people saw him, they recognized him as the man who used to sit and beg. The fact that they used the phrase *"used to sit and beg..."* means the man was no longer a beggar. His life had been transformed beyond imagination. The Bible says the people were filled with wonder and amazement at what had happened to the man. God wants to make you a wonder and amazement in your generation. He wants to transform you from one whom people used to turn away from, to one on whom they will look in utter amazement and wonder;

they will celebrate God's goodness in your life. As you apply the principle of change and the breaking of limitations shared in this book, the change that will come into your life will make people wonder. It will be the catalyst of change to those around you. This man's physical change and difference brought about a spiritual change and difference in the lives of many. Your breakthrough may be determinant in the breakthrough of countless others you do not know. You do not want to deprive others of their miracle because you would not pay the price for change and excellence. May those who have mocked you celebrate you because of the limitation that will be taken off your life! May those who have laughed at you rejoice with you! May those who hid from you come seeking the favor of God upon your life.

Summary

✱ The problem with many of us is that we end at the level of declaring, and proclaiming, and prophesying, and praying. Peter did something additional to the faith command he gave.

✱ The breakthrough you have been waiting for may be waiting on you. The miracle you have been expecting may be expecting you to make a move.

✱ God wants to make you a wonder and amazement in your generation.

✱ Your breakthrough may be determinant to the breakthrough of countless others you do not know.

✱ You do not want to deprive others of their miracle because you would not pay the price for change and excellence.

Part II

DEALING WITH UNPLEASANT & UNWANTED SITUATIONS

Part II: Dealing with Unpleasant & Unwanted Situations

Sometimes in life we all find ourselves in unwanted and unpleasant situations. Such circumstances seem to press hard on us, making us feel aching, humiliating, and deep seated desperation for which we seek relief. Many of us have been in such circumstances far longer than we thought or even imagined. The truth is for many, resignation to the backdrop of defeat, a sense of failure, anger and even resentment is where we find ourselves, thinking there is no way out. We have tried all we know but the issue seems to go nowhere. As we say it in Cameroon, it seems to be a *"come no go"* situation. In this part of the book, I want to share with you from my heart some strategies you can employ to get rid of unwanted situations. You can turn the tables on your circumstances. You can break free from whatever seems to hold you captive. You can break out of the siege the enemy has put you in or in which you have put yourself. I believe the solution to every human ordeal can be found in the Word of God. There are many stories we can draw a parallel to and glean from their wisdom to obtain solutions to problems that seem to plague humankind. Do you find yourself in a situation you consider unwanted and unpleasant? Do you long for freedom and breakthrough? Now I want you to get your Bible if you have one and turn to 2 Chronicles 32:1-21, or perhaps I should just copy the passage here so that I can be sure you'll read it:

> *1* After all that Hezekiah had so faithfully done, Sennacherib king of Assyria came and invaded Judah. He laid siege to the fortified cities, thinking to conquer them for himself *2* When Hezekiah saw that Sennacherib had come and that he intended to make war on Jerusalem, *3* he consulted with his officials and military staff about blocking off the water from the springs outside the city, and they helped him. *4* A large force of men assembled, and they blocked all the springs and the stream that flowed through

the land. "Why should the kings of Assyria come and find plenty of water?" they said. *5* Then he worked hard repairing all the broken sections of the wall and building towers on it. He built another wall outside that one and reinforced the supporting terraces of the City of David. He also made large numbers of weapons and shields.

6 He appointed military officers over the people and assembled them before him in the square at the city gate and encouraged them with these words: *7* "Be strong and courageous. Do not be afraid or discouraged because of the king of Assyria and the vast army with him, for there is a greater power with us than with him. *8* With him is only the arm of flesh, but with us is the Lord our God to help us and to fight our battles." And the people gained confidence from what Hezekiah the king of Judah said.

9 Later, when Sennacherib king of Assyria and all his forces were laying siege to Lachish, he sent his officers to Jerusalem with this message for Hezekiah king of Judah and for all the people of Judah who were there:

10 "This is what Sennacherib king of Assyria says: On what are you basing your confidence, that you remain in Jerusalem under siege? *11* When Hezekiah says, 'The Lord our God will save us from the hand of the king of Assyria,' he is misleading you, to let you die of hunger and thirst. *12* Did not Hezekiah himself remove this god's high places and altars, saying to Judah and Jerusalem, 'You must worship before one altar and burn sacrifices on it'?

13 "Do you not know what I and my fathers have done to all the peoples of the other lands? Were the gods of those nations ever able to deliver their land from my hand? *14* Who of all the gods of these nations that my fathers destroyed has been able to save his people from me? How then can your god deliver you from my hand? *15* Now do not let Hezekiah deceive you and mislead you like this. Do not believe him, for no god of any nation or kingdom has been able to deliver his people from my hand or

the hand of my fathers. How much less will your god deliver you from my hand!"
16 Sennacherib's officers spoke further against the Lord God and against his servant Hezekiah. **17** The king also wrote letters insulting the Lord, the God of Israel, and saying this against him: "Just as the gods of the peoples of the other lands did not rescue their people from my hand, so the god of Hezekiah will not rescue his people from my hand." **18** Then they called out in Hebrew to the people of Jerusalem who were on the wall, to terrify them and make them afraid in order to capture the city. **19** They spoke about the God of Jerusalem as they did about the gods of the other peoples of the world–the work of men's hands.
20 King Hezekiah and the prophet Isaiah son of Amoz cried out in prayer to heaven about this.
21 And the Lord sent an angel, who annihilated all the fighting men and the leaders and officers in the camp of the Assyrian king. So he withdrew to his own land in disgrace. And when he went into the temple of his god, some of his sons cut him down with the sword.

No one is immune to scenes like this in their lifetime. Such challenges which seek to bind and keep you in unpleasant situations and circumstances will always come at you in one form or the other. You must learn and master how to handle such situations so that your life can make a difference, firstly for you, and secondly for those around you. In our passage above, Hezekiah had just succeeded to bring reforms in Judah and to restore the Temple worship. Life in the land of Judah was returning to normal. The people had taken up the challenge of rebuilding their nation and returning to their God. For this, the enemy was not happy. He was pleased to see them going on in life in the miserable state they were found in. Immediately they made an investment for change, he came to pull them down to a state of slavery. Look at the opening statement of our passage above, *"after all Hezekiah had so faithfully done, Sennacherib invaded..."* This is the way of the enemy; whenever there is a reasonable investment for change he seeks to destroy it and render it ineffective. Do not expect that your desire for change will be respected by the enemy. Do no expect that your investments for change will be supported by the circumstances that seek to keep you in servitude. Each time you take a step to make a difference from your past there are forces that will seek to counteract what you do. To overcome such forces and make a lasting and permanent change from unpleasant and unwanted situations, you will have to understand the keys of victory and how to use them to effect necessary change whether at the personal, family or corporate levels. In the chapters that follow in this section, we are going to take a look at some of the strategies for making a change and a distinction.

Chapter IX

Know the Techniques of the Enemy

In our passage of reference, we find the nation of Israel in an unwanted and unpleasant situation because an enemy king had laid siege on Jerusalem with the intent of destroying it. Take note of all the techniques employed by the enemy forces to demoralize and defeat the Israelites:

He attacked their confidence (verse 10): *"On what are you basing this confidence of yours...?"* This question of the underling of the enemy king was meant to destroy the confidence of the Jews. Listen, be very careful with things and people who try to destroy your self-confidence and above all your confidence in God. The person with a destroyed self-confidence cannot stand in battle. The enemy is very good at this; he will first of all attack your self-confidence. This is to cause you to give up and give in to whatever it is that you do not want or find unpleasant. When you believe you cannot and take up a position of resignation, then no one can help you. Once he succeeds to destroy your self-confidence, his next target is your confidence in the God you are serving. The one whose confidence in God is destroyed is already done with! The one thing you should labor to guard in this battlefield of life is your confidence. You must have confidence in that which God has made of you and put in you. And above all you must have confidence in your God. If you can keep your confidence in tact, then you can make a difference and effect change from any unwanted and unpleasant situation.

He attacked their trust in their leader (verses 11&15): *"He is misleading you, to let you die of thirst and hunger…"* This was an attack on the people's trust in their leader, the one who could help them. The enemy often attacks your trust in those whom God has established to help you. As long as your trust is attacked and destroyed there is little hope for you to make it. It is important to trust those God has given to lead, counsel, and help you through life's hurdles. Never allow anything to destroy your trust in the leaders God has given you because God works through men. This is very important! If he succeeds to destroy your self-confidence, your confidence in God, and your confidence in those God has ordained to help you, then he has succeeded to keep you in permanent bondage. You will have to know and believe that the one seeking to help you is seeking your own interest and good. In this way you will be taking one step away from any unwanted situation and one step closer to your freedom.

He sought to belittle the God of the Jews (verses 14-15): If the enemy can get you to see your God through the eyes of the obstacle or situation, then he probably is on the verge of gaining the upper hand. If the enemy can cause you to believe that a particular situation is above the God you serve, then even God becomes "helpless" to help you (and I say it reverently). You must behold the situation and obstacle that lies before you through your God. When you look at things the other way round, then you are nowhere near your solution. Remember the twelve spies who were sent to spy out the land of Canaan?

Ten of them saw their God through the giants and two saw the giants through their God. Those who saw the giants through their God were those who came out of the wilderness, the others who saw their God through the giants perished in the wilderness. Never let anything dictate your perception of the God you serve, rather allow the God you serve to dictate your perspective of situations and circumstances.

He brought accusations against them (verse 12): This is another potent weapon of the enemy. The purpose of this weapon is to let you feel guilty and believe that you deserve the situation you are in because of one thing you did. The sad truth is that there are many of God's children whom the enemy has succeeded to make believe that God is against them. They are overwhelmed by a sense of guilt and unworthiness. As a result, they are tormented and refuse to seek help thinking if God is really against them then who can help them. You must understand God does not accuse or make you feel guilty; He convicts and brings you to a place of repentance and restoration. You must learn to reject all the accusations of the evil one and seek your freedom and liberty. Refuse to listen to the lies of the enemy. Even if you did something sinful, settle it quickly between you and your God by truly repenting and forsaking the sin. When that is done you must actively resist the accusations of the enemy which he rails in order to keep you bound.

He intimidated them (verse 18): The purpose of intimidation is to impose fear and terror. This is one of the greatest weapons of the enemy. He has often used fear and panic to defeat his victims. Fear is a trap and a poison that weakens and paralyzes. If your adversary can succeed to make you afraid, then he has succeeded to defeat you. Many dictators and satanists use this weapon to keep their victims under control. It is the same thing for those who find themselves in one form of addiction or another. They fear separation from their addiction thinking it is impossible to live without the addiction in question. Reject such intimidations and gain your freedom.

Now that we have seen the techniques and strategies used by the enemy to keep you in unpleasant and unwanted situations, we are going to look at what you ought to do to come out of such situations and keep yourself out permanently. For a review lets enumerate his techniques discussed above:

- Attack of self-confidence
- Attack of your confidence in God
- He sought to belittled their God
- Attack of your trust in those who can help you
- Accusation
- Fear and intimidation

Now we are ready to move on to learning how we can break free and gain permanent freedom from unpleasant and unwanted situations.

Summary

* Be wary of things and people that try to destroy your self-confidence and above all your confidence in God.

* If you can keep your confidence in tact, then you can make a difference and effect change from unwanted and unpleasant situations.

* The enemy often attacks your trust in those whom God has established to help you.

* If the enemy can cause you to believe that a particular situation is above the God you serve, then even God becomes helpless to help you.

* Never let anything dictate your perception of the God you serve, rather allow the God you serve to dictate your perspective of situations and circumstances.

* You must understand God does not accuse or make you feel guilty; He convicts and brings you to a place of repentance and restoration.

* Fear is a trap and a poison that weakens and paralyzes. If your adversary can succeed to make you afraid, then he has succeeded to defeat you.

Chapter X

Identify what is Feeding the Situation

We have spent the first section on this part of the book identifying the ways by which satan seeks to keep many in unwanted and unpleasant situations. Now I want to share with you from the same passage how you can break free from such circumstances, into God's abundant freedom for you. It is important that you understand the chronology of the strategy we are about to share. Many of us are still in unpleasant situations imposed on us by the enemy because we have applied our resources haphazardly, resulting in failure and defeat. Your first step to freedom and progress is for you to identify what is feeding the situation and cut off its supplies (verses 3-4). We are responsible most of the time for the things that seem to keep us in bondage for so long. You must come to a point where you are able to identify what is causing the unpleasant circumstance to thrive and destroy it. Hezekiah's first reaction was not to pray but to cut off the water supply of the enemy. What is it that is making your situation thrive? The Bible says, *"Can papyrus grow tall where there is no marsh? Can reeds thrive without water? While still growing and uncut they wither more quickly than grass"* (Job 8:11-12). If you search the scriptures you will find that papyrus and reeds are hiding places for leviathan and behemoth. In other words if there are papyruses in your life you must identify the marsh that is making them thrive. If you concentrate on cutting the papyrus without dealing away with the marsh then you are just creating a recurrent problem for yourself. As long as the marsh is still in place, there are greater chances that the papyrus will still show up. Same thing goes for the reeds, which signify instability and unsteadiness. Take away the marsh and the water, and the papyrus and reeds will wither. No more hiding place for leviathan and behemoth. This step cannot be compromised. All else you do will depend on this one vital step. You must cut off supplies!

Be Practical

If you have a problem with lust, what may be feeding the situation may be the kind of movies you watch or the company you keep. You must cut off the supplies in order to deal with it permanently, and perhaps seek for deliverance from spirits of lust. If your problem is drugs you will have to cut off contact with those who supply you with drugs or who feed your desire for drugs. If your problem is with debt, it means you spend far more than you make. This extravagance may be due to the fact that you have a strong desire for things you cannot afford. So to come out of the debts you have to deal with whatever is feeding such desires. It may be an illicit relationship you just must break in order to move forward. The Bible says even lions perish for lack of prey. That is, when there is nothing to feed on, no matter how strong the lion is, it will eventually die. In the same light no matter how strong and resistant the unpleasant situation you are in appears to be it will eventually become powerless and die thereby loosing its grip on you and letting you go. Many people try so hard to break free from what they spend their time feeding. I can only describe this as first degree folly. If all the energy and resources you waste in trying to break free were invested in cutting off the supplies of your unwanted circumstance you would have realized twice the victory you need.

The Need for Self-evaluation

I want you to write down any unpleasant situation you find yourself in. After doing this, write down what you think may be causing the situation to thrive. If there is more than one, write them down in the order of their influence on the situation. Now write down what you think must be done to cut off the supplies of what is feeding the situation in question. Take note that for different situations there may be different things feeding them. In some cases though, you may have multiple situations being fed by the same source. Whatever the case, you will have to identify them and take the necessary action. Remember, in part one of this book, we talked about the need to confront challenges. Now is the time to confront your first challenge and free yourself from any and every unwanted situation in your life. It will take hard work and persistence to completely cutoff the supplies. You need to be patient and steady in doing this. No room for wavering; this may only fortify the unpleasant circumstance.

Summary

* Your first step to freedom and progress is for you to identify what is feeding the situation and cut off its supplies.

* Many people try so hard to break free from what they spend their time feeding. I can only describe this as first degree folly.

* If all the energy and resources you waste trying to break free were invested in cutting off the supplies of your unwanted circumstance you would have realized twice the victory you need.

* If there are papyruses in your life you must identify the marsh that is making them thrive. If you concentrate on cutting the papyrus without dealing away with the marsh then you are just creating a recurrent problem for yourself.

* I want you to write down any unpleasant situation you find yourself in. After doing this, write down what you think may be causing the situation to thrive.

Chapter XI

Restoration and Repair

Once you have identified whatever is feeding the unpleasant and unwanted situations and cut off the supply of everything that was strengthening the grip of that situation of yours, the next step is to repair the broken portions of the walls of your life (verse 5). The broken portions of your life are those areas of your personality that have been wounded and negatively affected by the situation you were in. For example, if the situation you find yourself in is that of abuse due to emotional dependability inflicted on you by your abuser, after cutting off emotionally from him/her you have to learn to be emotionally independent. It may take some very hard work on your part. The broken and wounded parts of your personality, if not dealt with, will become entry points of the enemy that will make you return to the state of slavery. You cannot allow entry points for the enemy into your life and think he will not make his way in. Satan is a homeless vagabond seeking anywhere to lay his head. Don't make your life his address or playground by leaving open doors. Sinful compromise is what breaks our walls of defense against the enemy. You must identify the portions of the walls of your life which are broken, and do all in your power to repair them. Hezekiah did not go to pray until he had built up the walls around Jerusalem. He rallied his efforts and rebuilt the broken portions of the walls of Jerusalem because he was determined to keep the enemy out. He understood that he could never maintain freedom and the investments for change he had made by allowing broken portions which made it easy for enemy access. He was willing to do the hard work that was indispensable. Freedom and change do not come cheap, nor do they stay around cheap. It takes had work to obtain, sustain, and maintain them.

Areas in which you May Need Repairs

You may need to carry out emotional repairs if a broken heart was the open door to your unpleasant situation. You may need to repair your relationships if resentment, bitterness, and anger are the open doors to your bondage. You may need to repair your mind through sound teaching and meditation on the word of God if your situation was due to confusion of the mind and wrong doctrine or belief. You may need to repair your trust. For some people betrayal has caused their trust in everybody to be destroyed and hence they must rebuild their trust if they want to come out of where they are in. God will help you by using people, and if you cannot trust anyone, it will be difficult for you to be helped. You may need to repair your self-confidence and self-esteem. The bottom line is repairs are needed and must be done no matter the cost if change should be effected.

The broken walls may also be reflective of the areas of the Christian armor you may not have put on. Is there a portion of the Christian armor you have not put on, or which you have put off? It is time to put it back on! You may need to rebuild your faith in God through His word. You may need to rebuild your commitment in speaking the truth if you find yourself locked up in the prison of falsehood. Is there compromise in your life? Then you may need to put on the breastplate of righteousness. Whichever portion of this armor is lacking must be put on.

Summary

* The broken portions of your life are those areas of your personality that have been wounded and negatively affected by the situation you were in.

* The broken and wounded parts of your personality, if not dealt with, will become entry points of the enemy that will make you return to the state of slavery.

* You must identify the portions of the walls of your life which are broken, and do all in your effort to repair them.

* Freedom and change do not come cheap, nor do they stay around cheap. It takes hard work to obtain, sustain, and maintain them.

* The broken walls may also be significant of the areas of the Christian armor you may not have put on.

Chapter XII

Build Watch Towers in your Life

Once you have repaired the broken portions of the walls of your life, the next thing for you to do is to build watchtowers (verse 5). Watch towers are meant to be vantage points in your life from which you can spot the enemy from a distance. You must live your life in watchful observation. Know that you are in a state of war. After building such watchtowers, the next thing for you to do is to place sentinels on them. The sentinels can be personal indicators that raise a flag in your spirit when things begin to get bad so you can act in a timely manner and seek help before things deteriorate. Have your own personal security check and alarm system that will call your attention each time an intruder gets into your life. This intruder may be the spies that come on a reconnaissance mission to put you in bondage. Such security checks will tell you when a simple relationship is breaking the bounds of propriety and becoming inordinate. It will raise the alarm when a simple like for something is growing into a lust and eventually becoming an addiction.

In the book of Deuteronomy chapter four, Moses told the children of Israel at least twice to watch themselves closely so as not to allow the values of the surrounding nations to creep into their society. You have to watch yourself to ensure that your standards are not lowering morally and otherwise. In the book of Nahum we read, *"An attacker advances against you, Nineveh. Guard the fortress, watch the road, brace yourselves, marshal all your strength!"* (Nahum 2:1). The reason she was asked to guard the fortress and watch the road is to raise the alarm in case of enemy infiltration. Like I said before, just as depicted in the verse above, the enemy is always advancing against us to take captive one aspect of our life or the other. Watchfulness and alertness is what will keep him off. That is the reason for the watchtower you must build.

The Lord Jesus asked us to watch and pray. Many of us seem to pray without watching. No doubt we fail to identify demonic and satanic invasion. Ask the Holy Spirit to show you situations and circumstances the enemy is bringing your way. As such you can ward them off before they arrive. The purpose of watching is so you can pray. You must learn to approach the throne of grace to find help for yourself in times of trouble. No one can pray more effectively for you than yourself. Do not seek to enlist prayer support before you have prayed yourself. The whole New Testament is littered with commands and admonishments to watch yourself. This cannot be negotiated. Do you recall when Peter was walking on water towards Jesus? All the thrill and excitement of walking on the water did not keep him from being observant. It is true that he began sinking when he took his eyes off from the Lord to looking at the raging waves and panicked. However we should give him credit for the fact that in the midst of all that, he could notice when he began to sink and call for help. Many people fail to detect when they are slipping or drifting into the ravine of sinful compromise. They only come to their senses when it is too late to give them any meaningful help. The Lord could reach out quickly to help Peter before he sank because he called in time. Are you able to notice the first step in the wrong direction? I cannot give you exhaustive ways by which you can watch yourself. Because we all have different challenges in life you have to determine the means by which to watch yourself. You must determine what kind of security system to put around your personal life. In this way you will be making a difference in your life and effecting the change you need. In the book of Proverbs, the Bible says you should above all things guard your heart. Build a garrison around the things which are important in your life. You cannot leave them unattended to. However a garrison is not enough if there are no sentinels. And sentinels stand on watchtowers. For some people the watchtowers they build will be time limits to place on themselves on certain activities. For others it may be how much they spend on certain items. For some it may be certain thought patterns. Take time to watch and pray! Keep guard!

Summary

* Watch towers are meant to be vantage points in your life from which you can spot the enemy from a distance. You must live your life in watchful observation.

* Have your own personal security check and alarm system that will call your attention each time an intruder gets into your life.

* You have to watch yourself to ensure that your standards are not lowering morally and otherwise.

* The enemy is always advancing against us to take captive one aspect of our life or the other. Watchfulness and alertness is what will keep him off.

* You must learn to approach the throne of grace to find help for yourself in times of trouble. No one can pray more effectively for you than yourself.

* Many people fail to detect when they are slipping or drifting into the ravine of sinful compromise. They only come to their senses when it is too late to give them any meaningful help.

* Build a garrison around the things which are important in your life. You cannot leave them unattended.

Chapter XIII

Reinforce your Defense

We see that Hezekiah built another wall outside the existing one he had repaired (verse 5). By so doing, he was reinforcing his defense against enemy invasion. You can only effect change and make a difference when you have a strong defense system. Your defense determines how far you can carry your offense into enemy territory. Remember when the three and a half tribes chose to settle on the eastside of the Jordan and were required by Moses to have their fighting men march armed for battle before the rest of the Israelite army, the men requested to build walls around their city so that their families will be kept in safety. After they built the walls, they were gone several miles away for about seven years, yet returned to their families who did not come under attack because they were living in reinforced security.

For you, this will mean enlisting the help and prayers of others. Don't rush to this step while ignoring the first three. That is why many of us come to the point of saying the prayers of that man of God did not work. The man or woman of God cannot repair your walls for you nor can he build watch towers for you. All he can do is reinforce what you are doing. I have seen people moving from one place to another seeking help for that which they have to resolve to abandon; they are not yet determined to put in all that they've got to bring about the change that is needed in their life, yet they expect some other person to put in his/her all for them. It doesn't work this way my dear. You must understand that no lasting change or difference can be worked out in this way. If peradventure you happen to realize a change, it is going to be momentary if you have not cut off the supplies of what was feeding the situation, or have failed to repair the broken walls of your life, or worse still, have failed to identify the strategy of the enemy to put you in the situation you in which you find yourself. You cannot know permanent change until you build the necessary watchtowers in your life.

God works miracles and not magic! I have seen people in disappointment spread rumors about ministers of the gospel who have attempted to help them come out of one situation or the other. In a sense I blame such ministers who think they can help those who have refused to follow the steps necessary for total freedom. When I just started my deliverance ministry, I was so zealous to see everyone who came to me set free that, I would spend and expend myself to see them set free. It took time for me to realize that true freedom does not come by the determination of the minister but through the one needing the deliverance. If you provide reinforcement, and deliverance is obtained without the other vital steps in place, it is a matter of time before the person finds himself in a worse situation. Oh yeah, I have seen that happen again and again. Now I present the process of deliverance to the one seeking it and see how far he or she is willing to go with the first three stages before I can determine when to minister to the individual. Those who have been willing to go through the process and do their part have entered total freedom, no matter the bondage they were in. So, do not seek reinforcement until you have done the first three steps. It will save you a lot of time and energy, and may be even money and other resources. And of course it will save you from the embarrassment of unnecessary failure. There is no wisdom in trying when you know that failure is a hundred percent guaranteed. I am one of those who believe in trying even if the chances of success are extremely slim, but I do not attempt anything that is sure to fail.

Summary

* You can only effect change and make a difference when you have a strong defense system.

* Your defense determines how far you can carry your offense into enemy territory.

* A man or woman of God cannot repair your walls for you nor can he build watch towers for you. All he can do is reinforce what you are doing.

* Those who have been willing to go through the process and do their part have entered total freedom, no matter the bondage they were in.

* There is no wisdom in trying when you know that failure is a hundred percent guaranteed.

Chapter XIV

Arm Yourself

Hezekiah made a large amount of weapons (verse 5). As a believer you must know the weapons you have in your arsenal and use them against the circumstances you are not pleased with. I cannot mention all the weapons at your disposal. I have treated that topic in my book *"Triumphant Life"*. Here I will just mention the weapons you need in order to break free from unpleasant and unwanted situations. The number one weapon which you already have is the Name of Jesus. Like I said before, His Name is the most potent weapon you have to cause unpleasant circumstances to bow and give way. And you make use of this weapon through the avenue of prayer. Let's continue to look at the different arms you need to take up:

The Right Words

Speak the word of God to yourself and remind yourself of what your God can and will do on your behalf (verse 6): sometimes all you need to do is declare the power and might of your God. Declare what you believe He will accomplish on your behalf. Many people jump to this stage without passing through the first five; they think God is a magician. As you declare the word of God in faith, it begins to work for you, because God's word released in faith always accomplishes its purpose. In the book of revelation we read that, "they overcame him… by the word of their testimony." A testimony is not limited to what God has evidently done in your life but also includes what you believe He has done, can do, and will do. As used in the above verse in Revelation, this word can also mean testifying to what is going to happen. So you declare it and believe it. There is power in using the right words. In a sense, when David was before Goliath, the words he used were prophetic words of his testimony of what he believed His God was going to accomplish through him. You have to arm yourself with the Word of God, that which God has decreed about you. It is a mighty weapon to use against the enemy. The Bible calls the Word, the sword of the Spirit. Use it to cut yourself free from unwanted entanglements and ties to the past.

The Right Training

You may need to train yourself or better still seek training from someone willing and qualified to offer it on how to think the right thoughts, speak the right words, choose the right company, make the right investments, spend your money wisely, etc. Once you identify the areas you need training in, then go ahead and consult with the right person or group of persons who can help you.

Gain the Right Knowledge

It is often said that knowledge is power. What keeps many people in unpleasant and unwanted situations is ignorance, which is the lack of useful knowledge. So, one of the best ways to arm yourself is to seek knowledge that will help you. When you possess the right knowledge it will prove useful to you when you need it most. Do not despise opportunities to learn and acquire knowledge. This will require you to cultivate the habit of reading widely, especially in, but not limited to, areas where you are in need. The Lord declares in Scripture that His people perish for lack of knowledge as written in Hosea 4:6a, *"My people are destroyed from lack of knowledge."* Pay every possible price to gain useful knowledge. It will pay you dividends both in the long and short run.

It is only when Hezekiah had implemented all of the above strategies that God divinely intervened to rescue him and the nation of Judah from the predicament in which the king of Assyria had put them. May the Lord bless you as you put all this into practice and free yourself permanently from those unpleasant circumstances in Jesus' mighty Name!

Summary

✶ As a believer you must know the weapons you have at your disposal and use them against the circumstances you are not pleased with.

✶ The number one weapon which you already have is the Name of Jesus.

✶ Speak to yourself the Word of God and remind yourself of what your God can and will do on your behalf.

✶ As you declare the Word of God in faith, it begins to work for you, because God's word released in faith always accomplishes its purpose.

✶ The Bible calls the Word the sword of the Spirit. Use it to cut yourself free from unwanted entanglements and ties to the past.

✶ One of the best ways to arm yourself is to seek knowledge that will help you. When you possess the right knowledge it will prove useful to you when you need it most.

Part III

Avoiding Compromise & Mediocrity

Part III: Avoiding Compromise & Mediocrity

Compromise and mediocrity are the offshoots of indulgence and laziness, and those who must effect change and make a difference must actively work against the presence of such in their lives and in whatever domain they are responsible for. Indulgence and laziness are the graveyards of a great deal of potential, talent, and God-given ability slain by a lack of purpose and direction. In this part of the book, we are going to see how we can avoid compromise and mediocrity, so we can make a difference and effect a lasting change in our lives and environment. Our text of focus this time around will be from Genesis 19:15-30:

> *15* With the coming of dawn, the angels urged Lot, saying, "Hurry! Take your wife and your two daughters who are here, or you will be swept away when the city is punished."
> *16* When he hesitated, the men grasped his hand and the hands of his wife and of his two daughters and led them safely out of the city, for the Lord was merciful to them. *17* As soon as they had brought them out, one of them said, "Flee for your lives! Don't look back, and don't stop anywhere in the plain! Flee to the mountains or you will be swept away!"
> *18* But Lot said to them, "No, my lords, please! *19* Your servant has found favor in your eyes, and you have shown great kindness to me in sparing my life. But I can't flee to the mountains; this disaster will overtake me, and I'll die. *20* Look, here is a town near enough to run to, and it is small. Let me flee to it–it is very small, isn't it? Then my life will be spared."
> *21* He said to him, "Very well, I will grant this request too; I will not overthrow the town you speak of. *22* But flee there quickly, because I cannot do anything until you reach it." (That is why the town was called Zoar.)
> *23* By the time Lot reached Zoar, the sun had risen over the land. *24* Then the Lord rained down burning sulfur on Sodom and

Gomorrah—from the Lord out of the heavens. **25**Thus he overthrew those cities and the entire plain, including all those living in the cities—and also the vegetation in the land. **26**But Lot's wife looked back, and she became a pillar of salt.

27Early the next morning Abraham got up and returned to the place where he had stood before the Lord. **28**He looked down toward Sodom and Gomorrah, toward all the land of the plain, and he saw dense smoke rising from the land, like smoke from a furnace.

29So when God destroyed the cities of the plain, he remembered Abraham, and he brought Lot out of the catastrophe that overthrew the cities where Lot had lived.

30Lot and his two daughters left Zoar and settled in the mountains, for he was afraid to stay in Zoar. He and his two daughters lived in a cave.

The Scenario

To understand the above passage we must make reference to what preceded these unfortunate events. Prior to the destruction of Soddom and Gomorrah, Lot separated from his uncle Abraham, choosing for himself what he thought was the best part of the land and settling there. It was not very long before he found himself in the midst of a sinful and perverse generation. The city he thought was a place of safety was under impending judgment from on high. The truth is the place of apparent safety and security may pose serious spiritual risk. After the angels made known to Lot the intention of their visit and what was going to happen to those who dwelled there, he attempted to bring out his whole family including his soon-to-be sons-in-law but they did not take him seriously. And the Bible lets us know that when Lot was asked to hurry out of the city, he hesitated and the angels had to literally grab them by their hands to lead them out of the situation. Often when God wants to bring a change in our lives and have us make a difference, He demands that we make some *"sacrifice"* or take some risk. The truth is many of us spend too much time hesitating when it is time to make the determinant move that will bring change and make a difference. The question is, *"why did Lot hesitate?"* If we can answer this then we will see why we too often hesitate when it's time to make the determinant move. Let's now look at why Lot hesitated and how we can avoid this error.

Chapter XV

The Setback of Hesitation: Why we Resist Change

Hesitation is such a set back to progress that many fail to realize it causes more harm than the actual obstacles that may stand before us. When God says, "let go of this" hesitation is what will prevent you from obeying that instruction. If you must progress and bring change in your current situation, if you must move on to that which God is leading you into, you must deal a heavy and fatal blow to your hesitations. Knowing the reasons for hesitations will help you deal with it. From the above passage, we can bring out the following reasons why Lot hesitated:

The pang of separation

Though Lot had his wife and daughter with him, his sons-in-law had refused to follow and this caused Lot to hesitate. He was feeling the pain not only for himself but for his daughters who were losing their partners because of obedience to the command from the Lord. Lot was going to miss his neighbors and others with whom he related. He was going to miss his home and all that brought him comfort in his home. The human tendency to belong was having its toll on him, hence the hesitation. And the truth is, for most of us, it is the pang of separation that keeps us from making the necessary progress that will enable us effect change and make a difference. This pang may be due to separation from family members, friends, colleagues, neighbors, or any close relationship we may have built around us. We should know that those who have made the difference around them are those who have been willing to endure this pang of separation. Abraham made a difference because he endured the pang of separation from his family, and later from his concubine, Hagar, and first son Ishmael. But if he was to experience the change God was calling him into, he could not have bypassed this. To endure the cross and bring salvation to humanity, the Lord Jesus had to endure the pang of separation from the Godhead. He further endured the pain of being forsaken by the Father when He took upon Himself the sins of the world. We can go on and on; suffice it for us to stop with this list of examples. The pang of separation is inevitable if you must make a difference. It is time you asked yourself what separations you have to endure to bring change into your life and circumstances. Make up your mind to make the change happen by enduring the temporary pain necessary for effective and lasting change. For you too, change might imply your separation from a certain group of people who benefit nothing from you and from whom you benefit nothing. Some relationships exist only to bring loss and setback to those involved. The best thing is to kill such a relationship. Like I wrote elsewhere, the purpose of every relationship is the material, financial, spiritual, physical, emotional, mental, or intellectual wellbeing of at least one party involved, otherwise it is not worth it. You may have to leave the job you are working now and endure temporary pain and loss so you can bring a lasting financial or social change in your life.

The fear of loss

Sometimes taking a step forward will mean losing some things along the way, and often it will mean leaving some valuables behind. It is this fear of loss that makes many to stay in hesitation land and refuse to move to the next level. Often the things we hold so dear are the very things which hold us from making a difference and effecting change in our lives and surroundings. Sometimes, moving forward will require the loss of certain relationships. It may imply you losing your "reputation" before some people. It may require you abandoning the results of your hard work and investments. Lot hesitated because moving out of Sodom at that moment meant losing everything he had worked for and accumulated as wealth and property. Peter had to leave his profession as a fisherman to follow Jesus. James and John had to leave their father and profession to follow Jesus. Levi had to leave his lucrative business as a tax collector to follow Jesus. They were willing to accept loss and follow the Master who had called them. And of course we see the change that it brought to their lives and the difference it made to their world. Change often comes at the price of loss!

The Fear of the Unknown

The third reason Lot hesitated moving out of Sodom, was the fear of the unknown. The unknown usually comes with some degree of uncertainty, and it is this uncertainty that makes us want to stay in the comfort of the familiar. Change often requires stepping into the unknown and facing the uncertain. It was difficult for Lot to leave as long as he depended on the rationality of his thinking; all he had to do was to trust his God. About Abraham, the Bible says, *"By faith Abraham, when called to go to a place he would later receive as his inheritance, obeyed and went, even though he did not know where he was going."* (Hebrews 11:8) In other words it was his willingness to face the unknown and deal with the uncertain that caused him to bring change to his world.

Anybody who wants to make a reasonable and lasting difference or bring about a significant change must be willing to deal with these three issues raised: the pang of separation, the fear of loss, and the fear of the unknown. And the way we deal with these is by the simple act of trusting the Lord. Trust in God, and faith in Him and in that which He has said are the catalysts for lasting, permanent, and significant change.

We have seen the setback of hesitation and how to overcome it. Now we are going to look at some very powerful and world-changing instructions the angels gave to Lot and his family as they set out from Sodom. We will see how these instructions and commands can help us make the change we so desperately need in our lives, and make a marked difference from our yesterday.

Summary

* Compromise and mediocrity are the offshoots of indulgence and laziness, and those who must effect change and make a difference must actively work against the presence of such in their lives.

* Indulgence and laziness are the graveyards of a great deal of potentials, talents, and God-given abilities, slain by a lack of purpose and direction.

* The truth is your place of apparent safety and security may pose serious spiritual risk.

* Many of us spend too much time hesitating when it is time to make the determinant move that will bring change and make a difference.

* If you must progress and bring change in your current situation, if you must move on to that which God is leading you into, you must deal a heavy and fatal blow to your hesitations.

* It is the pang of separation that keeps us from making the necessary progress that will enable us effect change and make a difference.

Chapter XVI

Flee for your Lives

Another important virtue, yes I used the word virtue, is your ability to flee when you have to flee. Fleeing is not always a sign of defeat and failure; it sometimes is a sign of wisdom, discretion, and ultimately victory. It is not every battle you are called to fight, not every danger you are called to face, and not every risk you are called to bear. To effect a lasting change and make a permanent difference you must be able to choose your battles wisely. Take the essential risk, face the necessary danger but at the same time you must learn to flee from fighting useless battles and facing unnecessary dangers. Life is not and will never be a bravado competition determined by how much danger you can face or how much risk you can bear.

When the angels grabbed the hands of Lot and his family and took them out of Sodom, the first command or instruction to them was for them to flee. They said to them, *"Flee for your lives…"*

To flee is to run in a desperate, uncalculated, undignified manner from danger. When the Lord asks us to flee, it is because He knows that standing to face it will bring us nothing but defeat and failure. It is true that we have been programmed by our environment to believe that fleeing must always be associated with cowardice, weakness, and defeat. Yet we must understand that it is sometimes the gateway to freedom, safety, and victory. I have seen lives, ministries, families, businesses etc ruined because someone failed to heed to the command to flee. Let us look at some things you are commanded in the word to flee from:

Flee Sexual Immorality

Many lives, destinies, ministries, businesses, kingdoms, and empires have been ruined by this monster called sexual immorality. It is a monster that lurks closer than many are willing to admit first of all to themselves and to others. During the journey of the Israelites from Egypt to the Promised Land in one day alone the sin of sexual immorality destroyed over twenty-four thousand lives, more than all the other sins combined, and ruined countless destinies. This tells you the destructive power of this sin. God's recommendation or cure for this sin is to flee from it. The Lord has not asked us to resist, or to bind, or to cast it away. He recommends that we flee from it. Often it will show its ugly head in subtle and disguised ways, you have to be observant and flee when you see it show up. Writing to the church in Corinth Paul said, *"Flee from sexual immorality. All other sins a person commits are outside the body, but whoever sins sexually, sins against their own body"* (1 Corinthians 6:18). It is a sin no one is immune to unless the right precautions are taken. And the precaution the Lord recommends is fleeing. There are relationships you must flee from, some professions you must flee from not because they are evil in themselves but because they place you within reach and make you vulnerable to this monster of a sin. It means there are certain programs you will avoid to watch because they stir the feelings in you that attract the monster of sexual immorality. There are gifts and favors you refuse because they inhibit your capacity to refuse the advances of this monster. There are some open doors you will refuse to enter because you know the monster lurks on the other side of it. The wise heart is the one which says, *"Lord I will obey your Word and do what it says and flee"*.

Flee Idolatry

In the world today people will want to make you their idol or will want you to worship them; they want to become your god or make you their god. The Bible says you are to flee from this. This is another monster that has ruined many lives, destinies, ministries, kingdoms, and empires. Never give in to this powerful temptation that lurks so often in our societies today. Again Paul wrote, *"Therefore, my dear friends, **flee** idolatry."* (1 Corinthians 10:14) The apostle John puts it mildly, *"Dear children, keep yourselves from idols"* (1 John 5:21). Hence if you see where idolatry is practiced you are advised to keep yourself from it. Also you will have to watch that no system, person, or thing takes the place of God in your life, for if you allow it, that too will be idolatry. Do not accept to be a worshipper of another human being. That which takes the most of your time, resources, devotion, and so on may be an idol; reject it. Flee from idolatry.

Flee the Evil Desires of Youth

Writing to Timothy, Paul said, *"Flee the evil desires of youth and pursue righteousness, faith, love and peace, along with those who call on the Lord out of a pure heart. Don't have anything to do with foolish and stupid arguments, because you know they produce quarrels"* (2 Timothy 2:22). Paul was telling Timothy, there are things you must flee in order to fulfill your call to pursue righteousness, faith, love, and peace. The evil desires of youth are the desire for fame, power, unholy independence, extravagance, that which excites the flesh, useless adventure, the tendency to prove yourself right, and the like. All these are the desires of youth but in these modern days they seem to have become more the desires of adulthood!

Flee Persecution

Like I said earlier, it is not every battle you must fight. Some battles come to drain you and render you incapable of facing the ones that matter. So you must choose your battles wisely and face those ones that are necessary for you to move ahead. The Lord Jesus told His disciples that, *"You will be hated by everyone because of me, but the one who stands firm to the end will be saved. When you are persecuted in one place, flee to another. Truly I tell you, you will not finish going through the towns of Israel before the Son of Man comes"* (Matthew 10:22-23). By this, He was telling them to choose their battles wisely and to avoid fighting fights that do not matter. In fact there are some fights that are meant to keep you marking time, to have you stay in the same position. He demonstrated this several times by fleeing when the crowd wanted to stone Him. He could have faced the battles and call down angels to defend Him, but He knew by fighting these useless battles, He would reveal Himself as the Messiah and therefore the crucifixion for which He came would never had taken place. There was a time He purposely stayed away from Jerusalem because the Jews there were waiting to take His life (see John 7:1). Fleeing can be a strategy for victory. We see Joshua and the children of Israel used this strategy to gain victory over Ai. The rest of the tribes of Israel used this same strategy against Benjamin during the battle in which the latter was almost wiped out. Fleeing may be the gateway to your preservation. Moses fled from pharaoh into the desert were he was preserved until God's time of deliverance for the nation came. In the book of Revelation, twelfth chapter, we read that God caused the woman to flee from the dragon into a place in the desert He had prepared for her to be taken care of. So, fleeing can be a sign of wisdom, strength, preservation, and victory.

Summary

* Fleeing is not always a sign of defeat and failure; it sometimes is a sign of wisdom, discretion, and ultimately victory.

* It is not every battle you are called to fight, not every danger you are called to face, and not every risk you are called to bear. To effect lasting change and make a permanent difference you must be able to choose your battles wisely.

* Many lives, destinies, ministries, businesses, kingdoms, and empires have been ruined by this monster called sexual immorality. It is a monster that lurks closer than many are willing to admit first of all to themselves and to others.

* In the world today people will want to make you their idol or will want you to worship them, they want to become your god or make you their god.

* The evil desires of youth are the desire for fame, power, unholy independence, extravagance, that which excites the flesh, useless adventure, the tendency to prove yourself right, and the like.

* He was telling them to choose their battles wisely and to avoid fighting fights that do not matter. In fact there are some fights which are meant to keep you marking time, to have you stay in the same position.

Chapter XVII

Don't Look Back

The angles gave Lot and his family a second instruction wrapped in the same statement as the first. They told them to not look back as they moved out of Sodom to where the Lord was to lead them. Just like hesitation will keep you from stepping out, looking back will keep you from reaching your destination. If nothing else, looking back will slow you down and waste your time and resources. The reason the Lord placed our eyes ahead is so we can look forward always. Many people are held down and held back not by the present but by the past, what lies behind them. No one can truly look forward while looking behind him. And no one can truly move forward as he ought to if he keeps looking back. Paul said, *"Brothers and sisters, I do not consider myself yet to have taken hold of it. But one thing I do: forgetting what is behind and straining toward what is ahead, I press on toward the goal to win the prize for which God has called me heavenward in Christ Jesus"*. (Philippians 3:13-14). Notice that Paul said, *"this one thing"* which is forgetting what is behind and straining towards what is ahead. In order words you cannot separate your forgetting the past and your progressing forward. When you still hold to the past, you decided not to move forward. Many people wonder why they are unable to make a change from their past and move ahead, not knowing that it is impossible to move ahead while still looking back. The questions I want to answer in this chapter are, why do people keep looking back? What are the effects of looking back? And how can we prevent ourselves from looking back?

Why Do People Keep Looking Back?

There are several reasons why people keep looking back instead of taking forward strides towards change. Let's take a look at these.

What they Did to themselves

Some people are held back by what they did to themselves in the past. Because of this they have not forgiven themselves for what happened. They keep looking back at it and so cannot move forward. They are held back by self-inflicted guilt and refuse to forgive themselves. If you cannot forgive yourself who else will you forgive? They look back at:

- ◯ **The mistakes of the past:** This might be the mistake of a wrong choice, a wrong investment, a wrong move, or wrong purchase. There is no one who has lived his entire live without making any mistake. Those who have made a difference and effected change are not those who never made a mistake. The truth is, some mistakes are more costly than others, but you cannot keep looking back at them. Allow the grace of God to overshadow the mistake. It is true that some mistakes, you may have to live with your whole life, but your focus should be on how to use it to maximize your future. Regrets for past errors are no guarantee that you will not make those same errors if you do not transform your mind and move on with your life.

- **The failures of the past:** Past failures have the tendency to make you afraid to give another try, especially repeated failures. There are people who have succeeded after trying for the nth time. When you fail, find out why you failed and see what you can do to correct it; then move on and do not look back at the failure. It is not an act of humility to always look back to the failures of the past. If anything it is stupidity.

- **The sins of the past:** Another thing that can shade your view of the future and take your focus to the past is the sins of the past. This is the area most used by the devil to keep people from moving into their God-ordained destiny. The guilt of past sins can be so devastating if you have not learned to accept God's forgiveness promised in His Word. Every sin you have repented of has been covered by the blood of Jesus; do not allow the devil to use your past sins to keep you from entering the change God is working in you.

The above three things will keep you from moving ahead. There are people who see everything about the present and their future through the eyes of their past. And this keeps them from moving into their future or seeing the opportunities of the present. You cannot afford to view your present or your future through the eyes of your past. It will make you suspicious of your present opportunities and afraid to move into your future. Meanwhile, let us consider the second reason why people look back.

What OThers Did to them

What others did to us in the past can be described in one word as the hurts of the past. Many people live with past hurts for years, decades, and even a lifetime. Why allow your life to be ruined by someone else? Past hurts no matter the form they take can keep you stagnated and make your whole life ineffective. Past hurts may fall into any of the following categories:

- **Wounds of the past:** Wounds of the past can take the form of mental, emotional, and even physical wounds. Someone may have wounded you by his actions, words or attitude towards you. And this may cause you to live in a shell of self-withdrawal and build a wall around yourself that keeps others out and keeps you bound within the cocoon of resentment. If you live in such a state you must seek inner healing so as to move forward with your life.

- **Disappointments of the past:** you may have invested in something in your past and met with disappointment. It may be a business, a relationship or whatever venture you may have undertaken. And disappointments have the capacity to instill fear and paralyze an individual. My dear friend, you have to deal with any form of disappointment you may have had. I have seen parents disappointed by their children, and children disappointed by their parents. Either way, lives have been ruined by this, destinies crashed on the wall of moral failure, and hearts broken and shattered. I do not know how far or how deep your disappointment may be, but one thing I do know is that it can hold you back from fulfilling your destiny if you keep looking back to it. Resolve to part company with your past disappointments and press on to your glorious future.

- **Betrayals of the past:** I do not think there is anyone who has never been betrayed at least once in this life. People's love, trust, confidence, and favor have been betrayed, though to different degrees. This too can cause people to be held back as they refuse to love, trust, or confide in anyone because of the past. You cannot make a lasting change when you live in the disappointments of the past. Looking back to your past disappointments will blind you to your present and future appointments in life.

The Glories, Attractions, and Successes of the Past

Of course, it is not just the negative past which can hold people back. Some people are held back by the positive past; their successes, attractions, and glories of the past. As detrimental as the negative past is in your effecting a significant change and making a lasting difference, so can your positive past be. Some people are too caught up with the past that they fail to see the failures and disastrous mediocrity of the present. The best way to make a change is to compare the present with what ought to be instead of what it used to be. There are many people contented with the shadows of the past and so refuse to face the realities of the present. Also being caught up with what used to be can make you ungrateful for what God has done in your life, and for what He is in the process of doing.

The Ideas and Knowledge of the Past

It is very possible that the ideas and knowledge you had in the past that brought you success may no longer be relevant in the present. Your past methods that gave you an edge over your competitors in the past may place you at a disadvantage presently. To stick to such methods will mean being stuck in the victories of the past which may be defined as failures in the present. It is good to evaluate your past ideas and methods and see if they are still relevant so as to make necessary adjustments.

Why you should not look back

- **Looking back slows you down:** When you look back while trying to move forward, it slows you down and makes you waste useful energy.

- **Looking back makes you blind to obstacles ahead:** The probability that you will trip and fall is high when you try to move forward while looking back. Obstacles which will not make you fall if you were looking forward will do when you look back.

- **It prevents you from seeing present open doors:** When you concentrate on doors that were closed in the past, you will fail to see the ones which are currently open.

- **It makes you ungrateful for current blessings:** When you fix your gaze on the disappointments of the past it makes you blind to current blessings and hence you fail to give thanks.

- **It disqualifies you for service in the Kingdom** (see Luke 9:62).

- **Rear vision makes you lose focus of your destination:** The Bible says, "And let us run with perseverance the race marked out for us, fixing our eyes on Jesus, the pioneer and perfecter of faith" (Hebrews 12:1b-2a). As we look onto Jesus, we see both our future and essential past through Him. He is the screen to the future and the mirror to the useful and essential past. That is why we must see everything through Him.

We have come to the end of this chapter, but I want you to take some time to work on separating your mind and emotions from the past. Go into God's presence and ask Him to heal you of the wounds and disappointments of the past. Be specific in your requests. Separate yourself from the chains of the past that want to keep you tied to your past. Confess that you are marching forward into your destiny.

Summary

- Just like hesitation will keep you from stepping out, looking back will keep you from reaching your destination. If nothing else, looking back will slow you down and waste your time and resources.

- Many people wonder why they are not able to make a change from their past and move ahead, not knowing that it is impossible to move ahead while still looking back.

- Regrets for past errors are no guarantee that you will not make those same errors if you do not transform your mind and move on with your life.

- When you fail, find out why you failed, see how you can correct the problem, then move on and do not look back at the failure.

- Every sin you have repented of has been covered by the blood of Jesus; do not allow the devil to use your past sins to keep you from entering into the change God is working in you.

- Resolve to part company with your past disappointments and press on to your glorious future.

- Looking back at your past disappointments will blind you to your present and future appointments in life.

* The best way to make a change is to compare the present with what ought to be instead of what it used to be. There are many people contented with the shadows of the past and so refuse to face the realities of the present.

* It is good to evaluate your past ideas and methods and see if they are still relevant so as to make necessary adjustments.

Chapter XVIII

Don't Stop Anywhere in the Plain

The third piece of instruction that we find in the same statement as the ones in the previous chapters is, *"don't stop anywhere in the plain."* How can we relate our present discussion to the preceding instruction? The question we want to ask ourselves is, *"what does the plain signify?"* Why were they asked to not stop anywhere in the plain for any reason? What is the danger that lurks in the plain?

The plain is the place of worldly ease and comfort

The plain signifies our tendency to be given to worldly ease and comfort. This is one of the vices that keeps us from being at our best and effecting the most significant change and making a more permanent difference in our environment. The plain gives us a sense of false accomplishment and makes us feel we have already arrived. It is the place of comparison with that which others are doing instead of what one is called to do. On the plain people measure their success with respect to the failures of others instead of with respect to what they have accomplished in terms of what they are supposed to. The danger of the plain is that standards are dropped to suit the situation in question. When people are in the plain they cannot tell what standards to uphold because their values keep changing with respect to their circumstances. When you are in a plain, it is difficult to know when you are not making reasonable progress; hence life in the plain can be very deceptive.

You remember when Lot fist saw the plain at the time he was separating from Abraham? The Bible says, *"Lot looked around and saw that the whole plain of the Jordan toward Zoar was well watered, like the garden of the LORD, like the land of Egypt"* (this was before the LORD destroyed Sodom and Gomorrah). *"So Lot chose for himself the whole plain of the Jordan and set out toward the east. The two men parted company"* (Genesis 13:10-11). What Lot thought was the best choice he had made turned out not to be so. He thought the plain was going to be a place of security and safety for him; financially, materially, morally or otherwise but it turned out to be a place of immense danger and loss. In the plain you can be easily deceived by the appearance of things that present themselves to you. The plain is where opportunities are dived into without delving into where they will lead in the long run. Things and people are viewed as per what they can offer and the advantages they can bring now. The plain is the place of lack of proper vision. In the plain you appear to see very far but can't really tell the quality or details of what you see. Oh my friend, do not stop anywhere in the plain. One stop may be turned into a settlement. Avoid stopping in places which are not your final destination; the secret is to keep going. Do you remember the young prophet in the book of Kings who lost his life and ended his ministry? It was because he stopped in a plain to rest, and deception caught up with him.

The plain is the place of worldly and sinful compromise

I said before that in the plain there are often no standard values. Standards can be improved or dropped with respect to the situation. People in the plain are very flexible with respect to their handling of sin. Sin is coated and given names that seek to reduce the degrading nature of it. The language of people in the plain is marked by ambiguity; speech is equivocal. In the plain you are caught in the middle of nowhere. Do you know that it is easier to lose direction in the plain? Yes, because in the plain everywhere appears identical, so you can't easily tell when you are off track. We are told in the book of Genesis that, *"Terah took his son Abram, his grandson Lot son of Haran, and his daughter-in-law Sarai, the wife of his son Abram, and together they set out from Ur of the Chaldeans to go to Canaan. But when they came to Harran, they settled there. Terah lived 205 years, and he died in Harran"* (Genesis 11:31-32). Terah, the father of Abraham saw the need to make a difference; he wanted to bring a change in his life and environment and so he decided to set out for the hill country of Canaan. But we are told that when he came to Harran, which was in the plain, he decided to settle there. He compromised his goal for something else. He compromised his vision for what the plain was offering him and lost track of where he was supposed to be going. I believe God had called Terah to take his family from Ur to Canaan, but because he settled in the plain of Harran, God had to start over with his son Abraham. The fact that God called Abraham out of that place means that is not where they were supposed to be. Oh that you will not settle anyway in the plain! It may mean the end to what God has ordained for you.

The Plain is the Place of Vulnerability and Mediocrity

When there is danger of floods and the like, the first place to be affected is the plain. When an enemy army invades a land the first place they take over is the plain. The plain makes you vulnerable to defeat and failure. Plains are the opposite of mountains which have been known to be strongholds that provide refuge and safety in times of danger. When the enemies were seeking to stop the rebuilding of Jerusalem in the days of Nehemiah, after all their strategies had failed, the Bible says,

> *1* When word came to Sanballat, Tobiah, Geshem the Arab and the rest of our enemies that I had rebuilt the wall and not a gap was left in it–though up to that time I had not set the doors in the gates– *2* Sanballat and Geshem sent me this message: "Come, let us meet together in one of the villagesa on the plain of Ono." But they were scheming to harm me; *3* so I sent messengers to them with this reply: "I am carrying on a great project and cannot go down. Why should the work stop while I leave it and go down to you?" *4* Four times they sent me the same message, and each time I gave them the same answer.
> (Nehemiah 6:1-4)

The plain is enemy territory because it is the place of sinful compromise and worldly ease and comfort. The reason they invited Nehemiah to the plain was so they could have an edge over him since the plain would make him vulnerable to their attacks. They insisted four times with their request but each time Nehemiah turned it down; he understood that going down to the plain would mean descending to the level of the enemy.

The Place of Indecision

Another reason you should never stop in the plain is because the plain the also the place of indecision. Because things are never clear enough in the plain, it is difficult to make critical decisions. Change is the result of decision. Your decisions are what bring a difference in your circumstance, and the difference you make is what we call change. My friend, refuse to stop anywhere in the plain, it is not for you!

Summary

* The plain signifies our tendency to be given to worldly ease and comfort.

* The plain gives us a sense of false accomplishment and makes us feel we have already arrived.

* Avoid stopping in places which are not your final destination; the secret is to keep going.

* People in the plain are very flexible with respect to their handling of sin. Sin is coated and given names that seek to reduce the degrading nature of it.

* The plain makes you vulnerable to defeat and failure.

* The plain is enemy territory because it is the place of sinful compromise and worldly ease and comfort.

* Change is the result of decision. Your decisions are what make a difference in your circumstance, and the difference you make is what we call change.

Chapter XIX

Flee to the Mountain

The fourth and last simple, yet powerful instruction given to Lot and his family by the angels was, *"Flee to the mountains"*. The angels knew what it was going to take for Lot to run to the mountains, and in asking him to flee to the mountains, they were not asking too much from him and of him. The mountain signifies the place of excellence, the extraordinary, and the supernatural. But climbing the mountains takes total commitment and extreme hard work. It is not a feat for those who are given to ease and comfort. It is never a pleasure trip to climb a mountain because it demands all you've got mentally, emotionally, and physically. The truth is the Lord has called us into a life of excellence and extraordinary deeds and accomplishments. He has called us to inherit the life of the mountains. Many people shy from the mountains for several reasons which we are going to look at, but the most common reason why people fail to climb God's mountain is because they depend on their own strength and abilities. The prophet Habakkuk said,

"The Sovereign Lord is my strength; he makes my feet like the feet of a deer, he enables me to go on the heights" (Habakuk 3:19). To be able to climb the mountains the Lord wants you to climb you must come to know Him as your strength. You cannot depend on your strength to climb the mountain. The Lord will make your feet adapted to climbing and living on the mountain, and will enable you to go on to the heights of excellence, extraordinariness, and the supernatural. The psalmist, David said the same thing of the Lord:

> It is God who arms me with strength
> and keeps my way secure.
> He makes my feet like the feet of a deer;
> he causes me to stand on the heights
> (Psalm 18:32-33).

God wants to arm you with His strength and make you secure on the mountain. He wants to make you fleet footed to be able to run to the mountains, and when you have climbed to be able to stand on the heights. My dear, excellence is our heritage in Christ Jesus. If we pursue it God equips us and enables us to go get it. We are supposed to be go-getters of excellence and extraordinariness!

Why the Mountains?

Why does God ask us to dwell on the mountains? I want to share with you the blessings of the life of the mountains; remember the mountain signifies a life of excellence and extraordinariness.

The Place of Provision

When Abraham was asked to offer his son Isaac on the mountain, the Bible says he bound his son and was about to slay him when the Lord intervened and asked him not to do it. He was asked to look by and see a ram that the Lord had provided for the sacrifice. After this, it is written, *"So Abraham called that place The LORD Will Provide. And to this day it is said, 'On the mountain of the LORD it will be provided'"* (Genesis 22:14). Until Abraham reached the mountain of the Lord he did not experience God's provision for the sacrifice. If you want to experience supernatural supplies from above, dare to live on the mountain of God. The Bible says,

> They are the ones who will dwell on the heights,
> whose refuge will be the mountain fortress.
> Their bread will be supplied,
> and water will not fail them.
> (Isaiah 33:16)

Thus for those who dwell on the mountain, they have a continuous, abundant, overflowing, and extravagant supply of all they need, even beyond the supply of bread and water. This talks of constant provision of all your needs.

The Place of Refuge

We read above in the verse from Isaiah that those who dwell on the heights will have the mountain fortress for their refuge. The mountain is your refuge from a life of sin and compromise with worldly standards. It is the place of shelter from the enemy's onslaught. When you dwell on the mountain you are in a secure place beyond the reach of your enemies. The Lord Jesus Christ told the Jews that when they see Jerusalem surrounded by foreign enemies they should run to the mountains. This is because the mountain is a refuge for those who dwell there.

The Place of Instruction

The mountain is also the place of instruction. When God was to instruct Moses about the way of life for the Jewish people, He invited him to the mountain: *"The LORD descended to the top of Mount Sinai and called Moses to the top of the mountain. So Moses went up and the LORD said to him..."* (Exodus 19:20). Throughout the chronicles of Christian history, those who have dared to go the heights of total commitment and excellence have also been those who have had the privilege of receiving instruction from the Lord. Elijah was invited to the mountain of God where he received instruction as to his successor and other things he was to take care of before his departure. If you want instruction from the mouth of the Lord, you've got to leave the plain and go for the mountain life of excellence and extraordinariness. And remember the strength to climb the mountain is provided by the Lord.

The Place of Vision

The mountain is also the place of vision. Those who want to see clearly into the far distance climb the mountain to get a better view. When you are on the mountain of the Lord, you become a man or woman of vision. You see through the eyes of the Lord and therefore through the eyes of excellence. When the Lord wanted Moses to have a view of the Promised Land, he asked him to climb to the top of the mountain. The Bible says,

> *1* Then Moses climbed Mount Nebo from the plains of Moab to the top of Pisgah, across from Jericho. There the Lord showed him the whole land–from Gilead to Dan, *2* all of Naphtali, the territory of Ephraim and Manasseh, all the land of Judah as far as the western sea, *3* the Negev and the whole region from the Valley of Jericho, the City of Palms, as far as Zoar. *4* Then the Lord said to him, "This is the land I promised on oath to Abraham, Isaac and Jacob when I said, 'I will give it to your descendants.' I have let you see it with your eyes, but you will not cross over into it."
>
> (Deuteronomy 34:1-4)

Do you want vision? Go to the mountain and there the Lord will open your eyes to behold what He has in store for you.

The Place of Intercession

Those who want to make an impact on their world through the art of intercession also understand that you cannot separate intercession from the mountain life. In the midst of sudden attack from the Amalekites during their journey from Egypt, Moses assigned Joshua to lead the physical battle while he went up to the mountain to determine the battle from the heavenly perspective through intercession. And we read, *"Moses said to Joshua, 'Choose some of our men and go out to fight the Amalekites. Tomorrow I will stand on top of the hill with the staff of God in my hands'"* (Exodus 17:9). Of course the victory was won thanks to his intercession. When Elijah declared that there was going to be rain after the three years of drought, he went up to the mountain to intercede for the rain: *"And Elijah said to Ahab, 'Go, eat and drink, for there is the sound of a heavy rain.' So Ahab went off to eat and drink, but Elijah climbed to the top of Carmel, bent down to the ground and put his face between his knees"* (1 Kings 41-42). Elijah was telling Ahab to go do what people who live on the plain spend their time doing – eating and drinking, but he will go do what those who live on the mountain do – intercede.

The Place of Communion

Because the mountain is the place of sacrifice, the place of instruction, the place of intercession, and the place of vision, it is also the place of communion. The Lord did not just call Moses to the mountain to give him instruction, but primarily to have communion with him. He wanted Moses to feel His heartbeat for the nation of Israel. The Lord Jesus too went often to the Mount of Olives to commune with the Father. Elijah had Mount Carmel as the place of communion with his God. Those who live on the mountain have understood the importance of daily communion with the King, and so they take every blessed opportunity to meet with the King.

The Place of Revelation

The mountain is also the place of revelation. That is why it is the place of instruction, vision, provision, and communion. When you truly commune with the Lord, the byproduct is revelation. When the Lord Jesus wanted to reveal His glory to some selected disciples of His, we are told that He took them up a high mountain where He was transfigured before them and opened their eyes to see into the supernatural realm. Those who are willing and ready to pay the price of climbing the high mountain of God are those who receive the privilege of the revelation of Himself: *"After six days Jesus took with him Peter, James and John the brother of James, and led them up a high mountain by themselves. There he was transfigured before them. His face shone like the sun, and his clothes became as white as the light"* (Matthew 17:1-2).

We have seen why we must go the whole way to climb our mountain God is calling us to climb so that we can truly make a difference in our lives through the power of revelation, divine instruction, and intercession. But we see clearly that not all are committed to climb the mountain. Lot refused to flee to the mountains the angels asked him to flee to. In the next chapter we are going to see why people are afraid to climb the mountain of God and the danger of not climbing.

Summary

✶ The mountain signifies the place of excellence, the extraordinary, and the supernatural. But climbing the mountain takes total commitment and extreme hard work.

✶ The Lord will make your feet adapted to climbing and living on the mountain, and will enable you tread the heights of excellence, extraordinariness, and the supernatural.

✶ My dear, excellence is our heritage in Christ Jesus. If we pursue it God equips us and enables us to go get it. We are supposed to be go-getters of excellence and extraordinariness!

✶ If you want to experience supernatural supplies from above, dare to live on the mountain of God.

✶ The mountain is your refuge from a life of sin and compromise with worldly standards. It is the place of shelter from the enemy onslaught.

✶ Those who have dared to go the heights of total commitment and excellence have also been those who have had the privilege of receiving instruction from the Lord.

✶ When you are on the mountain of the Lord, you become a man or woman of vision. You see through the eyes of the Lord and therefore through the eyes of excellence.

* Those who want to make an impact to their world through the art of intercession also understand that you cannot separate intercession from the mountain life.

* Because the mountain is the place of sacrifice, the place of instruction, the place of intercession, and the place of vision, it is also the place of communion.

* When you truly commune with the Lord, the by-product is revelation.

Chapter XX

The Folly of the Negotiator

Lot refused to flee to the mountains as he had been commanded by the angels; instead he chose for himself a nearby city to which he decided to flee. In verses 18-22 we see Lot in the process of negotiating with the angels about the last command he was to follow.

18 But Lot said to them, "No, my lords, please! *19* Your servant has found favor in your eyes, and you have shown great kindness to me in sparing my life. But I can't flee to the mountains; this disaster will overtake me, and I'll die. *20* Look, here is a town near enough to run to, and it is small. Let me flee to it–it is very small, isn't it? Then my life will be spared."

21 He said to him, "Very well, I will grant this request too; I will not overthrow the town you speak of. *22* But flee there quickly, because I cannot do anything until you reach it." (That is why the town was called Zoar.)

(Genesis 19:18-22)

Your Excuses only Exclude you from the Exclusive

Lot gave every excuse why he was not to flee to the mountains. He was telling the angels they were being austere in asking him to flee to the mountain. He tried to let them understand how unfair that would be for him and his family to endure the ordeal of climbing to the mountain the Lord was requiring of them. Today we find negotiators everywhere in this life. They negotiate with themselves and convince themselves why they shouldn't give their all to a task. They negotiate the Word of God and choose which part of it they are to obey. They negotiate with the Holy Spirit which instruction they are to follow. One thing is sure, no matter the reason for your negotiation with divine instructions, I want to let you know that the negotiator has no spiritual future. Negotiation with God's word is the easiest way to resign from the onward call. Lot in the same breath said, "No" to a command while saying *"my lords."* He called them lords and refused to obey them. Are there not many people today calling Jesus Lord but refusing to obey the command of His Word? The Lord will not compel us to obey Him even if it is for our own good. It's our choice whether to render total obedience or to negotiate and render partial obedience. The angels granted to Lot his request to flee to the nearby little town of Zoar. He rejected the mountain of excellence for the plain of mediocrity. Because he depended on his own strength to climb the mountain, he forfeited God's plan for his life. My dear friend if you want to go far with God, refuse to negotiate with Him. The negotiator has no spiritual future! It is the human tendency to look at what is close enough, what is available and within reach instead of going for what God wants. Lot made his choice according to the nearness of the town he negotiated to flee to. The truth is the life of the negotiator is a miserable one. The thrill of extraordinary accomplishments is absent from the life of the negotiator.

Do not Wait until it's too Late

Though Lot had negotiated to go to this small town, after some time, for whatever reason, Lot with his daughters left the town. He realized, too late though, that you cannot know better than God. What God sees in the Zoar of your choosing, may take you a lifetime of wasted efforts and resources to discover. We read that, *"Lot and his two daughters left Zoar and settled in the mountains, for he was afraid to stay in Zoar. He and his two daughters lived in a cave"* (Genesis 19:30). Lot later realized that the safety and security he thought he was going to find in Zoar were lacking. We are told he was afraid to stay in Zoar. We are not told how long he stayed in Zoar or what terrified him. But we do know that Zoar was one of the cities of the plain that the Lord was going to destroy due to their wickedness; the only reason it was spared was because Lot asked that he be allowed to go and settle there. Every time when the Lord says this has to go, we must let go of it and not attempt to negotiate. The danger that the thing may pose in the future may not be known to us. There is an old adage that says all that glitters is not gold. What may appear to offer you success, security, fame, and fortune may be the very thing you will run away from. The sad thing is that you will never leave the same way you got into it. By the time Lot was leaving Zoar the moral standards of himself and his daughters had been tainted by the customs of the people of Zoar. Can I repeat myself here? The negotiator has no spiritual future. The first sign of a destiny that will be ruined is the tendency to negotiate the commands of God. The story of Lot that started so well ended in a moral mess because he refused to go all the way with God. Do not spare that which God has decreed must be destroyed. And do not accept anything short of what God is asking of you. This way you will avoid the folly of negotiation.

Summary

* Negotiation with God's Word is the easiest way to resign from the upward call.

* My dear friend if you want to go far with God, refuse to negotiate with Him. The negotiator has no spiritual future!

* The truth is the life of the negotiator is a miserable one. The thrill of extraordinary accomplishments is absent from the life of the negotiator.

* Every time the Lord says this has to go, we must let go of it and not attempt to negotiate. The danger that the thing may pose in the future may not be known to us.

Chapter XXI

Qualification for Life on the Mountain

Why are so many people afraid to climb the mountain? Or why do many find themselves incapable of climbing the mountain? These are the questions we will answer as we conclude this part of the book. I will like us to look at three separate passages in the Bible that deal with what it takes to climb and dwell in the mountain of the Lord:

> *1* Lord, who may dwell in your sanctuary?
> Who may live on your holy hill?
> *2* He whose walk is blameless
> and who does what is righteous,
> who speaks the truth from his heart
> *3* and has no slander on his tongue,
> who does his neighbor no wrong
> and casts no slur on his fellowman,
> *4* who despises a vile man
> but honors those who fear the Lord,

who keeps his oath
even when it hurts,
5 who lends his money without usury
and does not accept a bribe against the innocent.
He who does these things
will never be shaken.

(Psalm 15).

3 Who may ascend the hill of the Lord?
Who may stand in his holy place?
4 He who has clean hands and a pure heart,
who does not lift up his soul to an idol
or swear by what is false.
5 He will receive blessing from the Lord
and vindication from God his Savior.
6 Such is the generation of those who seek him,
who seek your face, O God of Jacob.

(Psalm 24:3-6).

14b "Who of us can dwell with the consuming fire?
Who of us can dwell with everlasting burning?"
15 He who walks righteously
and speaks what is right,
who rejects gain from extortion
and keeps his hand from accepting bribes,
who stops his ears against plots of murder
and shuts his eyes against contemplating evil–
16 this is the man who will dwell on the heights,
whose refuge will be the mountain fortress.
His bread will be supplied,
and water will not fail him.

(Isaiah 33:14b-16).

Psalm 24:3-6 gives us the requisite condition for climbing the mountain of the Lord; Psalm 15 and Isaiah 33:14b-16 give us the qualifications of dwelling on the mountain of the Lord. Remember we said the Lord enables us to climb to the heights and equips us to dwell on the heights. So it is one thing to get on the mountain of the Lord and a totally different affair to dwell on the heights. I believe we are not to be occasional and seasonal visitors to the realm of excellence, we are called to dwell there and make it our habitation.

Who can ascend the mountain of the Lord and dwell on the heights?

The following are needed for one to be able to climb the mountain of the Lord and to live on the heights:

- **Clean hands:** For you to be able to live a life that makes a difference, at least from God's perspective, your transactions have to be free of corruption. You must avoid using your hands for things that do not please the Lord.
- **A pure heart:** a pure heart is needed for one to be able to climb the mountain. You must purge your heart of sin and all forms of evil, and make a serious commitment to guard it from defilement.
- **Freedom from idols:** There should be nothing in your heart that has taken the place of God. There must be nothing that competes with your devotion to God. You must commit to nothing that competes with, or weakens your ultimate commitment to God.
- **Blamelessness:** You must keep yourself from inward and outward corruption. The holiness of God imputed on you by your confession of Christ Jesus should not be tainted by sin and worldly compromise.
- **Sincere truthfulness:** Your heart must be committed to truth and your mouth must speak truth. Anything that is not truth should be kept far from your lips. Have nothing to do with falsehood and its diverse subtle manifestations.

- **Speak evil of no man:** Slander is the speaking of evil about another. If you are to climb the mountain of God and stay there, you must commit yourself not to slander anyone.
- **Cast no slur:** To dwell on the mountain, you must not cast any slur on your fellow man. Make no disparaging remark of anyone. Treat no one as unimportant or non-existent.
- **Honor those who fear the Lord:** Your system of honor should never be based on what someone has or is, but it should be based on the fear of the Lord.
- **Integrity:** Your word should be your bond if you are to dwell on the heights. That is why those who live on the mountain of God do not speak carelessly, nor do they make promises thoughtlessly.
- **Honesty:** To dwell on the heights, your decisions should not be based on personal relationships, nor should they be based on what people have or can offer you. You must not take unfair advantage of others because of their circumstance.
- **Refuse to behold evil:** Those who must ascend and dwell on the heights must be those who refuse to behold evil with their eyes. They have shut the gates of their eyes to the entrance of anything that can defile soul or spirit.
- **Refuse to listen to evil:** Those who dwell on the heights speak evil of no one, and also refuse to listen to evil being spoken of anyone. They have closed the gates of their ears to the entrance of anything that defiles soul and spirit.
- **Walking righteously:** This means you do not use your feet to go anywhere that will bring defilement. That is why those who dwell on the heights do not just go anywhere. They are very selective of where they go to.

These are the qualifications of those who have access to divine excellence and extraordinariness. They are those who are used to make a difference in the heavenlies that effect change in the visible realm. May you be committed to climb to your mountain and to dwell on the heights of God; only then will you be able to make a difference and effect lasting change in your life and lives of those within your scope of influence.

Conclusion

As we saw throughout the pages of this book, change is possible from any and every situation in which you find yourself. Once you grasp the principles of lasting change we have shared here, every unwanted circumstance in your life can be dealt a fatal blow; every limitation can be overcome, and a lasting difference will made in your life and environment. Perhaps you have longed for change, and you have tried to do it all in your own strength. God wants to change you and help you effect the required change. The greatest and foremost change you need is to become a new creation. When you surrender your life to Jesus Christ and make a wholehearted commitment to Him, He changes you from the old man to the new. It is this internal change that will jumpstart the outward change you have always desired. Please pray with me if you have not yet made Jesus your Lord and Savior:

Lord Jesus Christ, I thank you for your love for me, and for dying for me on the cross. I acknowledge my sins and the need to turn away from them. Forgive all my sins, cleanse my heart and my life, and come and live within me. Be my Lord and my Savior. I give you my whole life; past, present, future. Help me Lord to make lasting change in my life and in my environment. In your glorious Name I pray, Amen.

Now change is in you, bring it out and change your world! God bless you.

Some Publications of Perez Publishing

www.ingramcontent.com/pod-product-compliance
Lightning Source LLC
Chambersburg PA
CBHW072336300426
44109CB00042B/1632